FOR AN INEFFABLE METRICS
OF THE DESERT

ALSO BY MOSTAFA NISSABOURI

Plus Haute Mémoire. Rabat: Souffles-Atlantes, 1968.

La mille et deuxième nuit. Casablanca: Shoof, 1975.

Approche du désertique ; précédé de *Aube*.
Casablanca and Neuilly: Al Manar, 1999.

Approach to the Desert Space. Translated by Guy Bennett.
Los Angeles: Mindmade Books, 2001.

MOSTAFA NISSABOURI

For an Ineffable Metrics
of the Desert

Edited by Guy Bennett

*Translated from the French
by Guy Bennett, Pierre Joris, Addie Leak
and Teresa Villa-Ignacio*

OTIS BOOKS

MFA WRITING PROGRAM
Otis College of Art and Design
LOS ANGELES ❘ 2018

Book design and typesetting: Heather John Fogarty

ISBN-13: 978-0-9860836-8-6

OTIS BOOKS
MFA WRITING PROGRAM
Otis College of Art and Design
9045 Lincoln Boulevard
Los Angeles, CA 90045

https://www.otis.edu/mfa-writing/otis-books
otisbooks@otis.edu

CONTENTS

NOTE ON THE PRESENT EDITION

This volume of the selected poems of Mostafa Nissabouri brings together writings from throughout his career, from early texts that initially appeared in *Souffles* in the mid-1960s to selections from a current, unfinished manuscript – *Divan de la mer obscure* [*Dark Sea Divan*] – still unpublished in the original French. With the exception of my translation of *Approche du désertique* [*Approach to the Desert Space*], until now the only complete work of Nissabouri's available in English, the trade editions of all of his books are out of print and difficult to come by. For this reason, yet no less for the pleasure of being able to share a broad selection of his work with interested readers, I am delighted that the present book has at last appeared.

For an Ineffable Metrics of the Desert includes more than half of Nissabouri's published poetry (and in the case of *Divan de la mer obscure,* of his hopefully soon to be published poetry, too). Texts were selected for their literary / poetic qualities, as well as for being representative of different facets of Nissabouri's work and its evolution as I perceive them (admittedly, subjective criteria and perceptions). Early poems such as "Des grottes ouvertes..." ["Caves open..."] and "Manabboula," which first appeared in *Souffles,* as well as his first book *Plus Haute Mémoire* [*Higher Memory*], were later included in revised versions in his second work, *La mille et deuxième nuit* [*The Thousand and Second Night*]; it is the later iterations of these texts that were translated for the present edition.*

---

* The initial published versions of the early poems, as well as other writings by Nissabouri, can be found in the *Souffles* archive of the Bibliothèque nationale du

Four translators, each with a deep committment to the promotion of North African and other poetries in English, have generously contributed to this volume. Their names appear on the section titles that include their work, and, when more than one translator has provided texts for a given section, their initials at end of each poem they have translated.

The volume concludes with an interview that I conducted with Mostafa Nissabouri via email in mid-2017. With so little information about the poet and his work readily accessible, his comments are invaluable for what they reveal of his personal literary history and activities, as well as for the light they shed on the socio-cultural atmosphere of Morocco at the time of its independence, and the role that literature and the arts played at that liminal moment.

It is my wish that readers who may be taken with Nissabouri's poetry, as I was when I first encountered it in the bookstore of the Institut du monde arabe in Paris in the late 1990s, seek out his books and other writings, read and share them, and in doing so contribute to the growing conversation about the work of this singular and inspiring poet.

— GUY BENNETT
Los Angeles, 2018

---

royaume du Maroc (http://bnm.bnrm.ma:86/ListeVol.aspx?IDC=3). Translations of some of them have been included in the recent anthology *Souffles-Anfas: A Critical Anthology from the Moroccan Journal of Culture and Politics,* Olivia C. Harrison And Teresa Villa-Ignacio, eds. (Stanford University Press, 2016). As for *Plus Haute Mémoire* as originally published, WorldCat shows only six copies available in libraries worldwide (http://www.worldcat.org/title/plus-haute-memoire/oclc/23400679).

La mille et deuxième nuit

THE THOUSAND AND SECOND NIGHT

1975 · EXCERPTS

❖

Translated by Addie Leak and Pierre Joris

Des grottes ouvertes pour la reptation de mes côtes comme si
j'étais comme si la ville et la grotte en moi
étaient séparées en ordinateurs chacun utilisant son propre
calcul poursuivant sa propre aventure de sillonnement de
    destruction et de rêve
de machines qui dépassent le temps de froids et de canicules
le temps dans notre tête enfouie sous chemise de vieux cancers
    de paradis
puisqu'on ne peut pas échapper à son destin
puisque c'est une question d'œil quelque chose de vivant
    quelque chose de tragique dans notre œil
puisque Sésame la grotte Sésame la ville toute ma cité émiettée
    comme sous le coup de réverbérations électriques et ma
    prière au volatile le grand maître enterré à Baghdad
la discorde de mes flacons de vapeur de lymphe détentrice de
    pouvoir d'ubiquité
que sirote
            le vampire
ni géographe ni géomètre n'ont pu donner d'explication au
    désastre qui m'a
jeté dans le kif
pas plus ces légendes entre les ruines qu'il
ne restera que moi
                        et moi je serai dévoré par un monstre
suis-je une ville reconstituée os après os ou suis-je une ville
éteinte ?
et qui mettra les lunes en grossesse, qui fermera le livre ?

CAVES OPENED...

Caves opened for the crawling of my ribs as if I were as if
the city and cave in me
were separated into computers each using its own system
pathfinding on its own a criss-crossing
    destruction and dream
and machines outstripping the time of cold and heat waves
the time in our heads layered under a shirt made of old cancers
    of paradise
since we can't escape our destiny
since it's a question of the eye something living
    something tragic in our eye
since Sesame the Sesame cave the city my society crumbled
    under the blow of electric reverberations and my prayer to
    the fowl the great master buried in Baghdad
the dissension of my lymph fume flasks holding the
    power of ubiquity
that the vampire

            sips

not geography nor geometry could give a reason for the
    disaster that
threw me into kif
no more these legends between the ruins saying that
only I'll be left

                and I will be devoured by a monster
am I a city rebuilt bone after bone or am I a lifeless
city?
and who will get the moons with child, who will close the book?

Ça fait rien, dis-je, si on me force presque quotidiennement à avaler le plat où l'on a disposé la mort de façon qu'elle soit végétale, et si la rue est d'anxiété. Je télescope. J'ajuste des rêves d'où a été propulsé mon cerveau en vastes bandes à peine perceptibles – des ondes – selon eux, et mon foie, selon moi. Ça fait rien si je ne réussis à saisir de l'abîme que les secousses symptomatiques et si localisés mes délires s'avèrent perceptibles sous forme de taches fuyantes – flaques de sang. Ça fait rien si mon anachronisme est à l'opposé de l'électron, l'électron et mon anachronisme constituant ce scandale d'accommodement à qui mieux-mieux d'où je soutiens que les transistors captent la voix des sirènes, les sirènes noires et blanches, pour capter la nuit, la nuit ainsi que toutes les caractéristiques de la lune ; et tu as les dents avec une petite fente qui ouvre dans mon imagination des lèvres de torpeur Tanit, et dans cette voyance un vieux tueur qui est le temps et dans mon rêve brusquement des motifs qui recommencent, ensablés, luxuriants, une foule pleine de territoires où je me mesure la ville la rue et moi sans que je parvienne à placer le coup décisif pour mettre fin à ce tressaillement Tanit, jetant ce rêve que la ville me renvoie parce que n'ayant jamais propulsé autant de têtes autant de doigts autant de portes et autant de poteaux électriques autant de chiffres d'héritages caravaniers ni été aussi tortueuse ni aussi impossible à atteindre du fait de la disposition des maisons qui la bordent basses arrivant à la gorge et du fait aussi des lampes électriques qui lui donnent un air de désert qui me rappelle que la nostalgie est une vertu du croissant lunaire, la nostalgie émiette, j'ai été émietté à force de me souvenir, émiettés les compagnons qui s'arrêtent afin de mieux chanter les départs à proximité de débris de maisons affirmant qu'il s'agit Tanit là d'un amour perdu d'une passion dévorante Sésame comme la nuit qui rassérène qui vient sans que je bouge sans réveiller une lune profonde difficilement reconnaissable

It doesn't matter, I say, if they force me almost daily to swallow the dish where they arranged death to make it vegetable, and if the streets are panic. I telescope. I adjust dreams from which they say my brain was hurled in vast bands barely perceptible – waves – and my liver, I say. It means nothing if I can seize only symptomatic tremors from the abyss and if up close my delirium is seen in the form of fleeting stains – pools of blood. It means nothing if my anachronism is the opposite of the electron, the electron and my anachronism constituting this scandal of settling each trying to outdo the other from which I say the transistors capture the voices of sirens, black and white sirens, to capture night, night along with all the characteristics of the moon; and your teeth have a little gap that opens in my imagination lips of Tanit torpor, and in this clairvoyance an old killer who is time and in my dream suddenly motifs that start again, stuck in sand, lustful, a crowd full of territories in which I measure myself the city the street and me without managing to strike the decisive blow to end this Tanit quivering, throwing away this dream that the city sends back to me because of never having hurled so many heads so many fingers so many doors and so many utility poles so many numbers of caravan legacies nor either been so twisting or so impossible to reach given the necklace of houses lining it low along the gorge and also given the street lamps that lend it a desert air which reminds me nostalgia is a crescent moon virtue, nostalgia crumbles, I was crumbled in remembering, crumbled the companions who stop to better sing departures from the nearby debris of houses affirming that it is Tanit all about a love lost a devouring passion Sesame like the night which calms which comes without my moving without waking a deep moon difficult to recognize

dans ce qu'elle a créé pour déclencher une apparence de temps immobile. J'avais une lune devenue masse spongieuse collant douars à moitié détruits d'où je n'ai rien pu retirer sauf un livre de descendances calamiteuses, moitié purulente moitié vagabonde. J'avais une lune dont j'ai été tétanisé n'ai pu la chasser même en appuyant des pouces depuis la tempe jusqu'au milieu du front de manière à faire sortir un point rouge entre les yeux, qui fait chavirer corps et corps, dans chaque articulation dans la moindre cellule ses relents de pestilence. Qui frappe. Qu'il y a nécessité de chasser vers les arbres, vers les dunes, et qui est porteuse de vieille rancune. J'avais une lune qui avait les dimensions de ma seule rêverie dans le ghetto des livres, dont je suis resté à tâter le grossissement
lent

     infernal

         ma voix boueuse

            collant au sabot de la mort

                  mon cerveau

avec les dimensions d'un champ de bataille où Sif ben Di Yazane aurait pu déterrer des centaines de scorpions d'or. Anémique, moi, me suis-je écrié. Moi et le reste dans les livres que viendra détecter le galactique occidental pour m'assurer de mon moyen-âge, de ma résurrection, de la beauté de ma religion, de ma jeunesse, mon primitivisme ma virilité mon sexe pitoyable, que c'est une question de temps, qu'il faut proclamer l'homme libre, que Berbère, que lui Barbare, que moi juif hindouiste fataliste fanatique et arabe, que lui Phaëton, qu'après tout nous ne sommes pas si différents sauf que lui correct, son chien, sa femme, son disciple qui n'a pas pu établir son passeport, roman à deux, kif, thé, je-délire-j'écris-en-tremblant-sous-le-coup-du-dé-lire, et Brahim dont il connaît la vie mieux que personne mieux que moi la Sicile Essaouira devant les petits ratons photogéniques éberlués comme par quelque nouvelle cataracte aux

in what it has created to bring about an appearance of immobile time. I had a moon become a sopping mass half purulent half roving clinging to half-destroyed douars that I could save nothing from but a book of calamitous descent. I had a moon that tetanized me could not chase it away even pressing thumbs from the temple to the middle of the forehead making a red dot between the eyes, which makes body and body capsize, in each joint in the least cell its stench. Moon that strikes. That it is necessary to chase toward the trees, toward the dunes, and that is the bearer of an old grievance. I had a moon with the dimensions of my lone reverie in the ghetto of books, whose swelling I have stayed to feel out
slow
     infernal
        my voice muddy
           sticking to death' s hooves
              my brain
with the dimensions of a battlefield where Sayf ibn Dhi Yazan could have dug up hundreds of golden scorpions. Me anemic, I cried out. I and the rest in the books that the Western galactic will come find to assure me of my middle ages, of my resurrection, of the beauty of my religion, of my youth, my primitivism my virility my pitiful sex, that it's a question of time, that the free man must be proclaimed, that Berber, that he Barbarian, that I Jewish Hindu fatalist fanatic and Arab, that he Phaëton, that after all we are not so different except that he is correct, his dog, his wife, his disciple who couldn't get a passport, novel à deux, kif, tea, I a m d e l i r i o u s I w r i t e t r e m b l i n g u n d e r t h e d e l i r i u m, and Brahim whose life he knows better than anyone better than me Sicily Essaouira in front of the little photogenic rats dumbfounded as though by some new deluge with

bruits fossiles écoutez-moi je suis prophète romain et en atten-
dant la révolution l'action d'abord l'action pour la galaxie et la
lune en moi puis la lune où je suis mes supplications lui plus
musulman que moi le prophète à Rome
avec des calculatrices électroniques en plein désert futuriste
avec une ville avec deux portes seulement
des pyramides des totems
des gens amoureux de la même vache que moi
dans cette ville je connais mon matricule
moi aussi
j'ai habité des déserts futuristes
moi aussi j'ai conquis la plupart de mes satrapies
j'ai avalé
des journées chaudes et j'ai ri
des fantasmes dans ma circulation sanguine et des cadavres
sans sépulture face à la ville à détruire et dont il restera une
autre ville que nous appellerons tous
                    Palmyre
et la grotte et le livre du doute
cinq hommes et le sixième un chien et moi le minotaure
et encore moi le minotaure la grotte six hommes et le septième
un chien et moi le minotaure
et encore la grotte six chiens six hommes et encore la grotte
un chien sans hommes et le chien apparaît avec l'effigie de son
absence
surtout la grotte à peupler de visions où traquer dans le rire
d'autres têtes de vaches dans des tas de rues ouvertes à même
les parois de l'antre séculaire du dormeur avec la vache la cité
d'airain sans passeport cordes machines oueds et caravanes
                    dans le rire
moi le minotaure et encore Tanit à point dans mes vapes
d'insomnie livresque et encore Tanit ses embryotomies
ses cuisses de courant d'air

fossil sounds listen to me I am a Roman prophet and in waiting
for the revolution the action first the action for the galaxy and
the moon in me then the moon in which I am my supplications
he more Muslim than I the prophet in Rome
with electronic calculators in full futurist desert
with a city with only two doors
pyramids totems
people in love with the same cow as me
in this city I know my ID number
I too
lived in futurist deserts
I too conquered most of my satrapies
I swallowed
hot days and I laughed
at fantasies in my bloodstream and cadavers without graves
facing the city to destroy and of which another city will remain
that we will all call
               Palmyra
and the cave and the book of doubt
five men and the sixth a dog and I the minotaur
and still I the minotaur the cave six men and the seventh a dog
and I the minotaur
and still the cave six dogs six men and still the cave a dog with-
out men and the dog appears with the effigy of its absence
above all to people the cave with visions in which to hunt down
in others' laughter cow heads in loads of open streets pressing
up against the walls of the sleeper's ancient den with the cow
the society of bronze without passport ropes machines wadis
or caravans
            in the laughter
I the minotaur and still Tanit immersed in my haze of booklike
insomnia and still Tanit her embryotomies her
gust of air thighs

et ma nuit appréhender la lune ne serait-ce
qu'y reconnaître mon cerveau fait d'écume seulement
ne serait-ce que ma pleine nuit
d'où je contemple des architectures

and my night catch the moon if only
to recognize in it my mind made only of foam
were it only my deep night
from which I contemplate the structures

AL

MANABBOULA

Pour que vous doutiez encore plus de nos origines
nous vous proposons des corps pour les usines-salut-de-l'humanité
sans ablutions
des corps tranquilles sur le sable les bureaux de placement
des corps tannés
                 l'histoire tuberculeuse
                         nous autres les chiens les perfides
nous autres au cerveau paléolithique les yeux bigles le foie thermo-
    nucléaire
des corps avec des tablettes en bois où il est écrit
que le sous-développement est notre maladie congénitale
          puis m'sieur
               puis madame
                   puis merci
sans oublier notre interminable procession de dents jaunes
et les vapes
notre sang moitié sang moitié arbre
des corps nourris de sauterelles et de pisse de chamelle
nous ne sommes pas
          même épileptiques
               dans les grottes de vos Platon
ni dans les contes de Shahrazade
pas dans vos statistiques sur la culture des peuples les maladies
guérissables par bouchée de petite ruine
                                  pas
dans vos bilans vos rapports frénétiques sur les grandes et inhumaines
    certitudes

MANABBOULA

So that you doubt our origins even more
we offer you bodies for salvation-of-mankind factories
without ablutions
bodies tranquil on the sand the placement offices
of tan-hided bodies
                    tubercular history
                              we others dogs traitors
we others with paleolithic brains squinty eyes thermonuclear livers
bodies with wooden tablets where it's written
that underdevelopment is our congenital disease
          then sir
                    then ma'am
                              then thank you
without forgetting our endless procession of yellow teeth
and the haze
our blood half blood half tree
bodies fed on locusts and camel piss
we are not
          even epileptic
                    in the caves of your Platos
or Scheherazade's stories
not in your statistics about different cultures diseases
curable with a mouthful of little ruin

                                        not
in your balance sheets your frenetic reports on the great inhuman
     certainties

ni les médailles
ni les cités de jade contre
nos refoulements

                                   nos stigmates purulents
nos matrices aboyant sous le vent
pas dans vos traités sur la biologie de l'homme pétrifié
bien que nous ayons
nos guerres fratricides
        et que
nous rêvions de planètes
de ruelles d'arcades de soleils au centre de la terre (nous connaissons
l'aliénation mentale et parlons de civilisations crevées mises à sac)
que nous vous accordions
au pied des murailles et murailles d'héroïne
les tétanos
les guerres d'estomac et de chacal
pour satisfaire votre esprit calculé sur les dossiers
de Rome et du Viet-Nam
vos lunettes de pèlerins nécrophages sur les remparts de Marrakech
nos rumeurs de foule démente mangeuse de caravanes
nos bidonvilles soleil sur soleil et djinns avec des allumettes
les épouvantails de nos fraternités – ah avec des oranges des fusils
    de siba
ah moi madame arrange vole pas moi monsieur bonne année bonne
    santé –
de toutes petites femmes avec de petites étoiles vertes sur le front
toute la légende pernicieuse de nos diaphragmes
toutes les affres du sang dans un vertige de mosquées-bidon et le frondes
nos corps
        affublés
             de tornades
pour conjurer vos corps tronçon hibernation
d'une petite névrose de sable nous-mêmes
sans kasbahs ni idiomes pas méditerranée-démence

or medals
or jade cities against
our repression

                           our purulent stigmata

our matrices barking in the wind
not in your treaties on the biology of petrified man
even though we have
our fratricidal wars
        and though
we dream of planets
of alleys of arched suns at the center of the earth (we know
mental alienation and speak of dead civilizations sacked)
and we grant you
at the foot of wall after wall of heroin
tetanus
wars of the stomach and of jackals
to satisfy your calculating mind on
the Rome and Vietnam files
your necrophagous pilgrims' eyeglasses on the ramparts of Marrakesh
our rumors of a demented caravan-eating crowd
our shantytowns sun on sun and djinns with matches
the bogeymen of our brotherhoods – ah, with oranges and siba
      rifles
ah ma'am me set up not steal not me sir have a good year good
      health –
tiny women with little green stars on their foreheads
the whole pernicious legend of our diaphragms
all the agony of blood in a vertigo of phony mosques and slings
our bodies
         saddled with
                tornadoes
to conjure your bodies section hibernation
of a little neurosis of sand ourselves
without kasbahs or idioms not Mediterranean insanity

pas
    mémoriser
réenraciner la mémoire
                cette grotte
                        cette chiotte
                                cette mort
courant les ruelles pieds et bras tatoués chewingum brosses à dents
avec des tas d'usines de phosphate des tas de livres
    des tas de rois et ça n'en finit pas de converser
dans
    des tas d'antres artificiels pour boire un thé magnifiquement
mérité brindilles sésame
et
    à ta santé la foule
bariolée qui changes de cap mais pas de lance
et qui changeras tout le long
    de tes pièges à rats
vieux meurtre inconditionnel qui nous aurais donné
contre un revolver tout un paradis de lubies
empilé sur nos échines mais alors
des tas de médinas
    pleines de coquelicots jusqu'à faire de nos ossements des vestiges de
    cités incomparables
l'oiseau
l'oiseau
et les voleurs d'oiseaux
barbare
            l'oiseau comme nos pérégrinations d'un arbre l'autre
jusqu'à l'arbre de violence qui nous passe par le corps
et vos mamelles maîtresses du sang vos mamelles nous n'aimons pas
la ville riant sous cape la ville sangsue non plus ses ères de nomad-
ismes et les sobriquets du soleil
ce malfoutu soleil qui n'en finit pas de tournoyer
et qu'on

not

    memorizing
rerooting memory
             that cave
                    that shitter
                            that death
running the alleys feet and arms tattooed chewing gum toothbrushes
with heaps of phosphate factories heaps of books
    heaps of kings and never-ending conversation
in
    heaps of artificial dens for drinking tea beautifully earned
sesame sticks
and
    to your health the colorful
crowd who will change course but not weapon
and who will change all along
    your rattraps
you old unconditional murder who would have given us
a whole paradise of whims stacked on our spines
for the price of a revolver but then
heaps of medinas
    full of poppies to the point of making our bones the vestiges of
    peerless societies
the bird
the bird
and the bird thieves
barbarian
             the bird as our peregrinations from one tree to another
to the tree of violence that passes through our bodies
and your teats mistresses of blood your teats we don't love the covertly
snickering city the bloodsucking city or its nomadic eras and the sou-
briquets of the sun
this fucked up sun that never stops whirling
and that we'll

chassera à coups de pierre
nous autres
    de timbales sur des nids de serpents pour fraterniser avec le sang
recouvrer la mémoire dans un orgasme de lunes
comme ces chameaux tranquilles qui nous envoient
    leurs saignées sur la poitrine
(saigne chameau de ton cou délirant
nous voulons
des chopes de sang qui écume
des caillots gros comme le poing accomplir
des voyages hélant le désert devenu poisson
saigne encore chameau saigne saigne
de cités pour les roses
tandis que les roses ont des crépuscules de Dadès
nous voulons dans ce sang
l'œil
    l'épée
dans ce sang pétrir la nuque du vent
violenter des seins et poursuivre
la foule jusque dans ta trachée artère
saigne chameau encore encore)

nous vous accorderons encore
des conspirations à la barbe de notre sexe
et pour compléter votre catalogue de superstitions
des mains
coupées
    désarticulées
des rues tête tranchée où nous avons pressé
toutes les humanités possibles contre nos poitrines terroristes
des rues
    pleines de cris de génisses flagellées d'écritures

chase away with stones
we others
*   with kettledrums on serpents' nests to fraternize with blood*
to recover memory in an orgasm of moons
like the calm camels who hit us on the chest with
*   their spurting blood*
(bleed camel from your delirious neck
we want
tankards of frothy blood
fist-sized clots to make
journeys hailing the desert turned fish
keep bleeding camel bleed bleed
societies for roses
as long as the roses have Dadès dusks
in this blood we want
the eye
*   the sword*
in this blood to knead the wind's nape
assault its breasts and pursue
the crowd into your windpipe
keep bleeding camel bleed bleed)

we'll still grant you
conspiracies right in front of our sex
and to complete your catalogue of superstitions
hands
cut off
*   dislocated*
streets head severed where we pressed
all possible humanities against our terrorist breasts
streets
*   filled with the bellows of heifers flogged with writing*

AL

PLUS HAUTE MÉMOIRE

1. Ce pourrait être quelque saignée que l'on pratique afin d'être
préservé des marches à travers l'aride

quelque arbre à merveilles
entre ce que je vis et ce que
je ne puis raconter. Ma mémoire
c'est des souks de tragique rébellion c'est des rues qui vont et
viennent

             et leurs entailles
c'est la foule ressassant de vieilles guerres à coups de couteau
tant que le siècle aura la dent fratricide c'est des croyances où
l'organisme entier vole en éclats et sans cesse reconstitué dû-
ment dressé en schémas obsessionnels
c'est les nomadismes l'arabe enterrant son cheval
des nomadismes qui font que d'une minute à l'autre
d'un millénaire l'autre nous voici en face de généalogies
d'arbres à fantômes

        par exode
           de petites peuplades étranges
des nomadismes qui rejettent
         tout alliage
            toute combinaison
c'est un continent sur lequel
il faudrait lever toutes les hypothèques de l'exil
   sans que j'échange ma tête contre celle d'un conteur public
sans gesticuler devant le prix de la menthe
pas
   en imagination

HIGHER MEMORY

1. It could be some blood-letting practiced so as to be sheltered
    from forced marches through the arid

    some tree of wonders
    between what I'm living and what
    I can't retell. My memory
    is souks of tragic rebellion streets that come and go
                                             and their incisions
    the crowd regurgitating old wars with knifings as long as the
    century will be fratricidal to the bone is beliefs in which the
    whole organism explodes into bits & pieces ceaselessly duly re-
    assembled under obsessional schemata
    is nomadisms the Arab burying his horse
    nomadisms that make that from one minute to the next
    from one millennium to the next here we are facing genealogies
    of tree with phantoms
                      by exodus
                                  of strange little tribes
    nomadisms that reject
                  any fusion
                                 any combination
    is a continent on which
    all the hurdles of exile should be cleared without me
        exchanging my head for that of a public storyteller
    without gesticulating faced with the price of mint
    not
        in imagination

ce pourrait être la fêlure par quoi j'atteins

                                       au profond
une autre zone forcée d'embouchures irréelles
qui pourrait exister dans des rêves mais je ne rêve
que parce que je veux changer
c'est une métamorphose opérée
sur chaque ville rayée de la carte
et sur chaque borne
précédant le désastre
c'est une fêlure, ma mémoire

d'invasions de tribus adoratrices du hibou et de l'Œil
(quoique je sois inénarrable) – c'est une fêlure dont je suis
le corps butin de sangs effrayants
c'est la foule qui comme une douleur m'empêche de marcher
dont je garde
jusqu'aux rengaines chamelières
c'est une réelle aventure que je ne transcende pas
en une quelconque somme de corps qui à peine touchés
     s'amassent en cités inaudibles

                                       je veux dire
corps pulvérisés
                  tous jetés à l'aveuglette
irrécupérables
               échoués au terme d'un voyage par syncopes de soleils
irrémédiablement autres
                    et absolument étrangers

je prends les maquis dans les cerveaux du temps tel que je suis
     grièvement nomade
je fais comme le typhon soufflant les pyramides va-t'en Pyra-
mide va-t'en ma mémoire va-t'en fleur des neiges va-t'en tes rois
tes reines esclaves et eunuques

it could be the crack through which I reach
                                        deep down
another forced zone of unreal embouchures
that could exist in dreams but I dream
only because I want to change
it is a metamorphosis performed
on every town stricken from the map
and on each milestone
preceding the disaster
it is a crack, my memory

of invasions by tribes worshipping the owl and the Eye
(even though I am inexpressible) – it is a crack of which I am
the body spoil of fearsome bloods
it is the crowd that like a pain keeps me from walking
of which I keep
even the camel drivers' ditties
it is a true adventure that I do not transcend
in an average sum of bodies that barely touched
        pile up in inaudible cities:
                                        I mean to say
pulverized bodies
                all discarded blindly
irrecuperable
                stranded at the end of a journey by sun stroke
irremediably other
                        and absolutely strange

I go underground in time's brains as I am grievously nomadic
I do like the typhoon blowing the pyramids go away pyramid go
away my memory go away snow flower go away your kings your
queens slaves and eunuchs

c'est

la plus haute des mémoires où se déclenche toute une lignée
   de juments
            sur lesquelles
                      à pris place
la mort maîtresse des murailles
j'ai choisi parmi les villes la ville la plus démolie
et la plus propice aux voyances
je pars dans ce matin incertain
je sens qu'une vraie douleur m'empêche de marcher
dans la reprise quotidienne du non-être
sphinx
      robots
             petites légendes d'infamie
                             se détachent
de mon corps qui ne trouve son accomplissement
                    ni dans les livres
ni par sortilèges
qui est complice dans l'érection des bidonvilles qui est mon
   corps sans ressources
je pars d'une fêlure
de minotaure pensif dans les citadelles blanches
de signalisations vers des cavernes autres
où ma réalité
est déhistorifiée
pas question de devenir
                    ou
                  d'avoir été
je suis une série de cavernes où se forgent toutes les mémoires
possibles

it is

the highest of memories where starts a whole lineage of mares
       on which

                rides

death mistress of ramparts

I have chosen among the cities the most destroyed city

and the one most propitious for visions

I walk away into this uncertain morning

I sense that a true pain is keeping me from walking

in the daily resumption of non-being

sphinx

      robots

           little legends of infamy

                      detach themselves

from my body that finds fulfillment

                neither in the books

nor in spells

that is an accomplice in the erection of slums that is my re-
    sourceless body

I start from the crack

of a pensive minotaur in the white citadels

of pointers toward caves that are other

where my reality

is dehistorified

to become

        or

          to have been

is out of the question

I am a series of caves in which all possible memories are

forged

2. *J'ai érigé des citadelles qui ont sombré*

sous le coup

de la maladie

dans d'énormes souterrains où s'amassent des siècles
d'errance

une civilisation simiesque

qui a fini par

me partager

la tête du corps

je me suis surpris à psalmodier

le rêve écarlate des grenades

mais aucune grenade n'arrivait à éclore sans engendrer
des nœuds gordiens des vautours pommes d'or
et des mers d'indicible amertume
je savais que c'étaient des citadelles bâties selon mon amertume
que c'étaient toujours ces rêves arrachés à même le sol sous forme de
chiens qui protestent
en signe de vieille querelle avec le monde
je savais que c'étaient les Nomadismes et me mis à engloutir jusqu'aux
limbes le roulement continuel des cités
je savais quels vents

m'avaient conçu

et pourquoi les vents ont le sang divinatoire
je me suis surpris à psalmodier le rêve écarlate des grenades

2.   *I have erected citadels that drowned*
                         under the onslaught
                              of sickness
          in enormous subterranean spaces where centuries of wanderings
          pile up
          an ape-like civilization
                    that has ended up
                         by separating
                              the head from the body
I surprised myself when I intoned
                         the scarlet dream of the pomegranates
          but no pomegranate managed to bloom without bringing forth
          gordian knots vultures golden apples
          and seas of unspeakable bitterness
I knew they were citadels built according to my bitterness
that it was always these dreams torn off at ground level in the shape
          of protesting dogs
as a sign of an old quarrel with the world
I knew it was the Nomadisms and started to wolf down all the way
          to limbo the continuous rolling of the cities
I knew which winds
                    had conceived me
                         and why the winds have divinatory blood
I surprised myself when I intoned the scarlet dream of the pomegranates

3. Mais doucement
    cette omoplate
    ces testaments illisibles
    ces yeux bandés et ces cœurs de caméléon
    mais doucement Damas dans mon poitrail
    Damas et ma nostalgie toute prête dans le hennissement du
        scorpion
    froide aiguisée
    Damas par flûte et timbale jusqu'à ma bosse de
        chameau fou
    pour rien
                    pour des cartes à jouer
    Damas de coccinelles dans ma fuite éperdue
    ô
    par quelle main rongée par la peste et quelle parole
    Damas déposée au fond de mon être
    accroupie bigle et rêveuse Damas chien de sang
    des rues des corps comme des rues avec des têtes de grives
    des myriades de corps à mon corps
    je suis un ogre qui dévore prince princesse ensuite jette leur
        palais dans un désert infranchissable
    n'oublie ni Baghdad qui nous a fait l'œil et le sourcil vénusiens
    ni cette fameuse bataille de Poitiers (ses anniversaires de
        fœtus mégots et ongles accrochés à l'importation)
    ni ton corps la foule et Damas si vieille que mon regard saigne
    ses amnésies purulentes
    son corps à mon épaule dans un petit sac délirant
    avec des you-you de libellule
    ô corps vampire les lobes atomiques où te mettre dans mon
        corps

3. But slowly
    this shoulder blade
    these illegible testaments
    these blindfold eyes and chameleon hearts
    but slowly Damascus in my chest
    Damascus and my nostalgia all ready in the scorpio's
        neighing
    cold honed
    Damascus by flute and timbale all the way to my mad
        camel hump
    for nothing
                    for playing cards
    Damascus of ladybugs in my headlong flight
    oh
    by what hand gnawed at by the plagueand by what language
    Damascus sedimented at the base of my being
    hunkered down cross-eyed and dreamy Damascus blood dog
    streets bodies like streets with the heads of thrushes
    myriads of bodies to my body
    I am an ogre devours prince princess then throws
        their palace into an impassable desert
    forget neither Bagdad which made our eye and brow Venusian
    nor that famous battle of Poitiers (its birthdays of fetuses
        cigarette butts and nails hung on importation)
    nor your body the crowd and Damascus so old my gaze bleeds
    its purulent amnesias
    its body against my shoulder in a small delirious bag
    with dragonfly ululations
    oh vampire body the atomic lobes where to put you into my
        body

mon corps saignée homme-non-civilisation-homme-sauterelle
mon corps de toutes les reptations vers l'éclatement du jour
kasbah au petit vent des métamorphoses
mon corps tu saignes tu baignes dans une eau d'étrange pluie
    qui te fait jujubier
troqué pour les humanismes de strangulation
mon corps
le sang pourtant comme une tornade et tu dors
mon corps araignée aux yeux multiples
arbre de drogue mon corps entre chameau qui a faim et
    chameau qui a soif
ils
nous fouillèrent le corps pour y verser de petits
    gobelets de sang
afin que nos corps
restent à tournoyer sous leur soleil arthritique
chien après chien
nous poussèrent à la rue le corps bandé de linge humide
n'oublièrent
ni les fibules
ni les coutelas au poignet
nous accordant le sursis de la mémoire
une grotte où enfumer des corps chargés d'amulettes
n'oublièrent
       ni les tôles
           ni les petites pentes sous la lune
ni la faim
      pratiquée
         menstrues
              par la nuque

my body a blood-letting no-civilization-man-grasshopper-man
my body of all the reptations toward the explosion of day
casbah in the gentle wind of metamorphoses
my body you bleed you bathe in a water of strange rain that
    makes you jujube tree
exchanged for strangulation humanisms
my body
and yet the blood like a tornado and you sleep
my body a spider with many eyes
tree of drug my body between hungry camel and
    thirsty camel
they
body-searched us to pour in small
    goblets of blood
so that our bodies
keep whirling under their arthritic sun
dog after dog
into the street we pushed the body wrapped in wet linen
forgot
neither fibulas
nor wrist knives
granting us memory's reprieve
a grotto in which to smoke the bodies laden with amulets
forgot
    neither the sheet metal
                nor the little slopes under the moon
nor the hunger
        practiced
          the menses
               through the nape

4. *nous avons indéfiniment rêvé, accrochés aux arbustes, d'une femme qui en nous apercevant agiterait les manches — rivage sans rivages ; qui offrirait des langues d'hirondelles à notre patience femme qui s'accaparerait la lune pour en faire entre ses seins une mosquée blanche, entre ses seins des crans d'arrêt, femme sur les murs conquis vêtue de prescience en touffes d'arganiers pour de nouveaux voyages, cette femme jetait ses flûtes et la ville dévorait la femme*

   elle est celle qui alignait des pierres sur son ventre, étalée au sol, et se proclamait hibou l'année de famine

   nous avons rêvé accrochés au dernier espoir, de toi femme dans la demeure fraîche d'une ultime sagesse ; après chaque migration tu étais le carrelage qui reposait la rotule éprouvée, et la voix démantelée qui n'a pas fait son pèlerinage

   notre ancêtre fit sa guerre d'égoutier quand le
   haschich avait l'œil du faucon

   nous avons fait de toi femme le livre qui initie aux hautes solitudes et à la colère, nous avons tous crié dans la nuit cette nouvelle découverte de ton corps aux prismes de multitude, la foule et ses tambourins autour de la ville qui n'en finissait pas d'applaudir

   et qui montait

   gambadant

   sautillant

   flanquée sans ossements d'une chanson de porte à porte et d'une poignée de sel où dort l'héritage narcotique de quelques misérables brancards nous en sommes devenus épave errante dont tu es le paysage aux roses tourmentées, ô femme, et contre quelques boulettes d'ambre nous voici à fumer une cigarette sur les cadavres que nous pourrions être avec toute la logique et toute la science et tout le savoir qu'un cadavre peut maintenir au niveau de ces combats abstraits qui n'ont rien à voir avec les dimensions du continent sanguin

4. *we have dreamed indefinitely, clinging to the shrubs, of a woman*
who, seeing us, would wave her shirt sleeves—shore without shores;
who would offer swallows' tongues to our patience woman who would
appropriate the moon to make of it a white mosque between her
breasts, switchblades between her breasts, woman on the conquered
walls dressed presciently with argan boughs for new journeys, this
woman threw away her flutes and the town devoured the woman
she is the one who aligned the stones on her belly, flat on her back,
and proclaimed herself owl the year of the famine
we dreamed, clinging to the last hope, of you woman in the cool
dwelling of a last wisdom; after each migration you were the tiling
that rested the weary kneecap, and the dismantled voice that hasn't
done its pilgrimage
our ancestor did his sewage worker war when
hashish had the eye of the falcon
of you woman we made the book that initiates into the high solitudes
and into anger, we all screamed in the night this new discovery of
your body with its multitude of prisms, the crowd and its tambou-
rines around the city that couldn't stop applauding

                    and that rose

                              gamboling

                                   hopping

flanked without bones by a door-to-door song and a handful of salt
where the narcotic heritage of a few miserable stretchers sleeps we
have become its erring wreck of which you are the landscape with
the tormented roses, oh woman, and against a few pellets of amber
here we are smoking a cigarette on the corpses we could be will all the
logic and all the science and all the knowledge a corpse can maintain
at the level of these abstract battles that have nothing to do with the
dimensions of the blood continent

ô femme
retrouvée dans la passe violente d'une mémoire et d'un sexe violents
nous t'avons proclamée haut, dans nos conflits avec le sable et l'eau et
proclamée dans notre apostasie, fait de toi la suprême interrogation

oh woman
found again in the violent trick of a violent memory and sex
we have highly proclaimed you, in our conflicts with the sand and
the water and proclaimed in our apostasy, made of you the supreme
interrogation

Mais doucement
à l'écrit du sable et les complots de mon squelette
la foule ma petite tempête à la jeune blessure de tes sarisses que je
promène
        sans sourciller
tes bracelets simiesques et tes mains en pousses de nèfles pour faire
        circuler la monnaie d'incommunication
tes liseurs d'aisselles accrochant des biles contre le mauvais œil l'œil
les dunes dans ma voix saharienne
tes voix de cartomancienne dans les ruelles
dans tous ses appels au plus offrant
et la guerre qu'on n'oublie point sur le tabouret des vaines attentes
et le vent mystifiant tes tatouages dans une romance idiote
et ce rêve interminable où tu es en camisole de force
et tes mamelles et jusqu'à la secousse de ton ventre mon vrai nom
un fétiche néolithique à morsures
                            à tes orgasmes de vieille foule
sur les trottoirs en clameurs et une caverne où
un homme qui n'a plus de nom décline son nom à un homme
                    derrière un homme
                            derrière d'autres hommes
        à tes fientes tes idiomes que je parle sans connaître mon vrai nom
                            c'est toi qui déracines
je suis
        ton ossature sismique le miracle animal de tes fables
moi guerrier lacustre aspergeant la mer de coriandre
sans généalogie aucune
                            moi l'oiseleur
je téléphone à tous les morts je leur dis
taisez-vous bande de salauds
je suis un téléphone constamment branché sur les foules

But slowly
to the sand's writing and my skeleton's conspiracies
the crowd my little tempest to the young wound of your sarissas that
I take for
   a walk without raising an eyebrow
your ape-like bracelets and your hands like loquat shoots to help the
   coins of incommunication circulate
your readers of armpits hanging bile against the evil eye the eye
the dunes in my Saharan voice
your fortune-telling voices in the side alleys
in all its calls to the highest bidder
and the war one does not forget hunkering on the footstool of un-
   availing waiting
and the wind mystifying your tattoos in an idiotic romance
and this interminable dream in which you are in a straightjacket
and your teats and all the way to the tremor of your belly my true name
a neolithic fetish with bites

                      to your old crowd orgasms
on the clamoring sidewalks and a cave where
a man who no longer has a name spells his name to a man
            behind a man

                   behind other men
   to your droppings your idioms that I speak without knowing my
   true name

                    it is you who uproots
I am
   your simiesque bone structure the animal miracle of your fables
I lacustrine warrior spraying the sea with coriander
without any genealogy

                   me the bird-catcher

I phone all the dead and tell them
shut up all you bastards
I am a phone continuously plugged into the crowds

45

je suis

la nuit du Destin je suis Simbad et son génie terrien revenus à la
vie de cyclope

je te trafique un passeport pour mes songes te donne le tartre de mes
dents les latrines
et je chien
une arme à la main

I am
destiny's night I am Sinbad and his terrestrial genius come back to
cyclops life
I counterfeit a passport to my dreams for you the tartar of my teeth
the latrines I give you
and I dog
weapon in hand

5. Nous ne sommes jamais revenus. De cité en cité il y avait nous et nos brancards de héros morts en plein rêve d'amour et auxquels nous avons consenti tous les assortiments de la gloire : tapis, encens, bijoux, jamais nous n'avons enjambé le sang, fût-il celui d'un coq, pour ne pas être sujets à malédiction. Nous les berçons, infiniment, après leur avoir réservé une grotte dans notre minotauromanie de bienséance ; nous ne les évoquons pas non plus : ils sont là et nous les écoutons.

De cité en cité, d'île en île
nous irons à l'île de Ouaq-Ouaq
    où pas un oiseau ne vole
    où pas un animal ne bouge
    nous irons à l'île de Ouaq-Ouaq
    pour des provisions d'amnésie
    (remplis ô remplisseur et remplis un oued vide)
    à l'île de Ouaq-Ouaq gloire à l'amnésie
    frappe-moi la tête à coups de pierre
délire ma main délire qu'on en finisse avec les prénoms luna-tiques qui nous font peu à peu des parentés avec l'angoisse puis deviennent son œil noir par l'œil les princes la ville on-cle chacal ses fraternités de sarcopte et de poussière dans les effondrements
délire mon ombilic sur les cadrans solaires de mon corps de flèches de bouées délire comme à l'avancée du crotale noctam-bule et comme j'avais pris la pomme et la femme qui égrenait la légende de ses seins musqués dans les bas-reliefs les menhirs et quand je draâ dans mes vertèbres de foule assise dans une détresse de cheveux plaqués foule planque foule fille de joie que j'emmure au-dessus des échauffourées et des luttes

5. We never came back. From city to city there was us and our stretchers of heroes dead in a dream of love and to whom we have accorded all glory's miscellany: carpets, incense, jewelry, never did we step across blood, not even that of a cockerel, so as not to fall prey to malediction. We cradle them, infinitely, having reserved them a grotto in our minotauromania of decorum; we do not conjure them up: they are here and we listen to them.

From city to city, from island to island
we will go to the island of Ouaq-Ouaq
    where no bird flies
    where no animal moves
    we will go to the island of Ouaq-Ouaq
    to stockpile amnesia
    (fill up oh filler-upper and fill up an empty oued)
    glory to amnesia on the island of Ouaq-Ouaq
    hit my head with stones
hallucinate oh my hand hallucinate so as to be done with those lunatic first names that slowly ally us in kinship with anguish then become its black eye through the eye of the city's princes uncle jackal his fraternities of itch mites and dust in the disintegration
hallucinate oh my navel on the sundials of my body of arrows of buoys hallucinate as at the progress of the night-erring viper and as I had taken the apple and the woman who said one by one the legend of her musky breasts in the bas-reliefs the menhirs and when I draâ in my vertebrae of a sitting crowd in a distress of matted hair crowd hides crowd call girl I wall in above the scuffles and the tribal

tribales de mes sangs
délire et proclame ton délire de vieille foule
thaumaturge
        vieille renarde
           dans nos squelettes d'intempéries
délire au-dessus des mosquées qui nous valurent un sexe
irrationnel
que je me fasse des corps auxquels insuffler tes mémoires doubles
tes mythologies vénériennes te réduise
à une sacoche de sable
             aveugler
                    les passants qui voyagent
délire tu te dépeuples nous sommes prisonniers
d'une histoire avortée
je t'ai
moi-même crachée
           ensuite hélée
               puis tressée dans une insulte
nous sommes frères
à la mort
frères
les bras en barbelés et sans cesse à créer toute une humanité de
vertige et au nom d'un hibou et d'un sang
    et d'une besace où nous enfermer
pour les curiosités non-esthétiques l'exotisme d'exploitation
foule gang
pour une géographie scabreuse dans nos pensées quand nous
échangeons vêtements et babouches cuites et désespoirs
des larmes d'infidélités
              villes
            rosaces
               braises

affrays of my bloods
hallucinate & proclaim your hallucination of old crowd
thaumaturge

      old vixen

         in our bad weather skeletons
hallucinate above the mosques to whom we owe an irrational
sexuality
that I create for myself bodies into which to breathe your double
memories
your venereal mythologies that I reduce you
to a bag of sand

      to blind

            the traveling passersbys
hallucination you become depopulated we are prisoners
of an aborted story
I myself
spat you out

      then hailed you

         then braided you into an insult
we are brothers
onto death
brothers
arms in barbed wire and ceaselessly to create a humanity of
vertigo and in the name of an owl and a blood line
   and a saddlebag where to shut us away
for the non-aesthetic curiosities exploitation exoticism
crowd gang
for a scabrous geography in our thoughts when we exchange
clothes and slippers drinking bouts and despairs
tears of infidelities

        cities

         rose windows

           embers

délire sur le haut et au bas des murailles
tu as des breloques et des images
   pour mes épopées
         transhumante
              à l'image d'une boule d'os
                      grelottante avec des
poupées en plastique et des bagages de terrains vagues je te vois
pas même en rampe tu bégaies tu te fais un ventre obèse
pour épater les touristes
comme si tu n'avais plus de
alors que tu es ce corps impossible à conquérir
si ce n'est par la seule vertu de la parole
qui se crée sans cesse
          et comme si tout était fini
et qu'il faille recommencer à bâtir avec d'autres corps
d'autres semblants d'humanités
      tracer d'autres frontières
jeter d'autres sorts
écrire d'autres livres où il est question
du même prochain
         avec le même turban
les mêmes moineaux pour fêter je ne sais encore quelle lune
clamant moléculaire
mais délire
tant de villes au détriment d'un démêlé de villes qui naissent
   et ne naissent pas
au hasard de notre histoire que tu voudrais jalonnée de boî-
   tes d'allumettes
que tu veux obsession sur obsession sur défaite que je veux
corps jusqu'aux mythes d'une foule à tête de taureau, incalcu-
lables ampoules dont les vibrations ébranlent le cerveau de la
mort

hallucinate on high and at the foot of the walls
you have trinkets and images
   for my sagas
         transhumancing
               in the image of a ball of bones
                        shaking with
   plastic dolls and vacant lot luggage I see you
   not even in the limelight you stammer you make yourself an
   obese belly to impress the tourists
   as if you had no more
   though you are this body impossible to conquer
   if it isn't the only virtue of the word
   that creates itself ceaselessly
         and as if everything was done with
   and it was necessary to start rebuilding with other bodies
   other semblances of humanities
            to trace other borders
   cast other spells
   write other books mentioning
   the same next of kin
               with the same turban
   the same sparrows to celebrate I don't yet know what moon
   molecular lulling
   but hallucination
   so many cities to the detriment of a tangle of cities that are
      born and are not born
   by the chance of our history that you'd like punctuated by
      match boxes
   that you want obsession after obsession after defeat that I
   want to be a body all the way to the myths of a crowd with
   a bull's head, incalculable bulbs whose vibrations rattle
   death's brain

la mort est dans le plus simple de tes attirails, ô foule (tasse de café,
miroir dents en or et l'asphalte pour les petits frères). Voici encore
les caftans de paille les cortèges la danse du ventre voilà que les rues
nous traversent nous nous comprenons nous savons
combien nous sommes non pas séparés

                              mais brisés

                                   jetés
dedans nous-mêmes et les grottes où nous n'avons ni père ni mère
sauf quelques cailloux compte-gouttes de sang pour trancher une fois
pour toutes cette question de cataclysme dans le corps et dans le sys-
tème nerveux

                    ni toi

                 ni moi

                    n'avons à nous épargner insultes révolutions
vitres cassées arbres arrachés bidonvilles et sexes en érection macabre
nous nous aimerons plus fort

death is inside the most simple of your accoutrements, oh crowd
(coffee cup mirror gold teeth and asphalt for the little brothers). Now
here also the straw kaftans the processions the belly dance now that
streets cross us we understand each other we know
how many we are not separated

                but broken

                  thrown

into it ourselves and the caves where we have neither father nor
mother except for a few pebbles blood drops by drop to decide once
and for all this question of cataclysm in the body and the nervous
system

                neither you

                  nor I

                    have to spare insults revolutions
broken windows torn up trees slums and sexes in macabre erection
we will love each other more

6. Sous ton aisselle la mort je me suis mis à fabriquer d'autres
   foules au-delà à chaque coin de rue je créais un homme il me
   suffisait de lui dire marche pour qu'il marche Puis le désert Puis
   un trou Puis moi devenu le maître du sang/son hibou   Mon
   corps était millénaire je l'ai
                                isolé
retranché dans sa propre multitude afin de te donner entre
toutes les villes de la plus interdite à la plus réfractaire à mes
prières
comme Babylone sur le grand bovidé monté par la fille aux serpents
comme Grenade sensiblement éprouvée par les générations
      humides
et Marrakech aux tergiversations anales
je croyais échapper à ces malédictions mais toutes les poulies
des mots n'ont pas réussi à désancrer en moi cette autre foule
qui tétanise, qui est au-delà des mots et des formes, qui fait par-
ler couleuvres, coquillages, arbres, signes que je voudrais en-
cercler d'un grand mur et qu'elle reste dans ses rêves dans ses
ruines ses langues à demi-mortes la foule dont j'ai dressé des
centaines de cartes géographiques recourant au seul baroud lu-
naire de ses chevauchées dont j'ai fait égouts cassures
      œil et main suspendues
                                entre moi et mon corps
la foule devenue le douar ameuté sous les sauterelles
et la ville qui complote
inconséquente dans ses siestes
à en devenir soi-même l'araignée
qui dévore la ville

6. Under your armpit, death I started to produce other crowds
beyond on each street corner I created a man it was enough
for me to say to him walk and he'd walk Then the desert Then
a hole Then me becoming the master of the blood/his owl My
body was thousands of years old I isolated

                                                    it
entrenched in its own multitude so as to give you among all
the cities from the most forbidden to the one most defiant of
my prayers
like Babylon on the large bovid ridden by the serpent girl
like Granada markedly tried and tested by the humid
     generations
and Marrakesh and it anal procrastinations
I thought I'd escape these maledictions but all the word pul-
leys didn't succeed in unachoring in me that other crowd that
tetanizes, that is beyond words and forms, that makes garter
snakes, shellfish, trees talk, signs that I wanted to encercle with
a large wall so that it stay in its dreams in its ruins its half-
dead languages the crowd of which I've created hundreds of
geographical maps with recourse to only the lunar battle of its
cavalcades of which I made sewers breakages
     eye and hand suspended
                              between me and my body
the crowd having become the roused douar under the grasshoppers
and the city that conspires
inconsequential in its siestas
to thus become itself the spider
that devours the city

7.   ô foule
      je prends sur moi toutes les fuites hilaliennes cependant qu'à
      l'autre bout de mon corps
      Damas
      a déjà fermé ses portes
      je ne le dis à personne j'en fais un pigeon qui roucoule matin et
      soir et je répète je suis l'Euphrate je suis la pierre le vacarme et
      la fosse de lapidation
      je suis de cette foule le foie irascible de corps éparpillés qu'il fallait
                                  rassembler

                                                souder les uns aux autres
      toute une humanité dont nous ne connaissons
      que les peaux de timbales pour le chant du damné
      diagnostiqués selon
                      le typhus
                              et la chasse aux portugais
      et notre sang électronique branché sur une ère
      qui donne
      sur Gog
              et Magog

7. oh crowd
   I take upon myself all the Hilali flights
   though at the other end of my body
   Damascus
   has already closed its gates
   I don't tell anybody I turn it into a pigeon that coos morning
   and evening and I repeat I am the Euphrates I am the stone the
   racket and the lapidation ditch
   of this crowd I am the irascible liver of scattered bodies one had to
                              gather
                                        weld one to the other
   a whole humanity of which we know only
   the drum skins for the song of the damned
   diagnosed according to
                      typhus
                              and the hunt for portuguese
   and our electronic blood plugged into an era
   that gives
   on Gog
        and Magog

8. Au-delà des mots et des formes
    le reste se résume en quelques contes qui s'en vont par l'oued
        l'oued
    pleins de bâtonnets de sucre ne cessant jamais de fondre :
    un
    qui aurait perdu son œil à la suite d'une aventure où il s'agit
        d'un cheval noir enfermé derrière une porte en or
    l'autre
    engoncé dans les cernes d'un peuple fataliste
    Je pourrais dire c'est moi m'écrier miracle je pourrais m'en aller
        sans mot dire
    j'ai frappé mon corps de mobilité et sa mémoire de bassins de
        mouvance
    tel le cerveau de la rue qui éclate dans ses propres murs
    tel son cœur transpercé de minarets aux voix
    de démence dans vos demeures
    quelque gisement secoué de paresses fabuleuses
    l'omoplate
    la vision
    et la parole qui ressasse indéfiniment un peuple pointant sur
        toutes vos villes
    l'obscénité de son médius
    et tel ces villes-rougeoles
    ces villes détruites dont je suis le dépositaire des trois cent
        soixante-six sagesses de la mort
    dans ma longévité
                        tonitruante.

8. Beyond the words and the forms
    the rest can be summed up in a few tales that drift away in the
        oued the oeud
    full of little sugar sticks that never stop to melt:
    the one
    who's supposed to have lost his eye following an adventure
        involving a black horse locked behind a golden door
    the other
    enfolded in a fatalist people's eye bags
    I could say it is me could yell miracle I could leave without
        saying a word
    I beat my body into mobility and its memory into basins of
        movements
    like the brain of the street that explodes inside its own walls
    like its heart transpierced by minarets with demented voices in
    your dwellings
    some deposits shaken by fabulous lazynesses
    the shoulder-blade
    the vision
    and the words that indefinitely dwell on a people pointing over
        all your cities
    the obscenity of its middle finger
    and like those measles-cities
    those cities destroyed for which I am the depository of the three
        hundred sixty six wisdoms of death
    in my thunderous
                        longevity.

PJ

Nuits de l'Art qui deviez revenir depuis que vous
    êtes une attente
pour qui cherche un arbre de nudité
des nuits de luth enchantent l'eau qui passe
sous la plante du pied

Vous qui deviez retentir pour qu'un muezzin dans
    ma vieille ville natale
lentement redresse la pyramide
adopte un démon vert et consacre aux anges une coupole
qui deviez rendre possible l'art et possible l'ivresse
faire du rêve une colombe
qui nous ramène des flocons blancs
                          depuis les neiges du Liban
revigorant nos squelettes chancelants écrasés par le ciel

Qui deviez nous livrer dans un coffre sans serrure
le sol et ce qu'il renferme et les divisions sept de l'éther
entretenir notre préciosité avec tapis et sofas sans pareil
pour qu'en ouvrant le coffre
vous soyez la clairvoyance du regard et l'intuition de la main
qui souvent nous égare

Marée ténèbre vent suicide
nous restituer toutes les horloges au cadran de nopal

OH NIGHTS OF ART…

Oh Nights of Art meant to return since you
    became an expectation
for whoever seeks a bareness tree
nights of lute enchant the water passing
under the sole of the foot

You who were meant to resound and help a muezzin in
    my old birth city
slowly straighten the pyramid
adopt a green devil and consecrate a cupola to the angels
you who were meant to make art possible and drunkenness
possible
fashion from dream a dove
who brings us white flakes
                              from the snows of Lebanon
reviving our staggering sky-crushed skeletons

You who were meant to deliver us the earth and its contents
and the seven divisions of the ether in a box with no lock
maintain our affectation with peerless carpets and sofas
so that in opening the box
you become the clairvoyant gaze and the instinctual hand
which often leads us astray

Tide darkness wind suicide
give us back all the clocks with their nopal faces

qui firent la gloire de nos turbans et notre cœur à
    hauteur de l'épée
Dans votre opacité vous êtes un miroir
vous savez notre sang célèbre par ses mauvais voyages
vous nous savez merveille d'un désert de cécité
tant nos femelles furent ces régénératrices de citadelles
    blanches
où quand j'étais poète
j'ai de par mon sang renversé sur une pierre
moi aussi proclamé déesse une biche qui s'abreuvait sous le
    palmier

Vous savez notre catastrophe nos détresses nos
    pays en flagrant séisme
séisme de la tempe et séisme du regard impulsant
    le naufrage
vous savez quelles ruines et quelles angoisses rendent
    nos yeux beaux
vous savez nos préservatifs contre les rues à gages nos impasses
fratricides quand le jour des querelles nous achetons à la criée
toute généalogie qui lèvera le séquestre

Vous savez de quelle terre impérieuse et de quel tombeau vide
nous sortons nos pérégrinations nos âges menaçants notre Doute
et cette enfance
pleine de jeunes chiens coupés au rasoir pour nous savoir
reclus agonisants
Vous savez et je ne mettrai pas de jasmin dans les rues
je n'élèverai pas de mausolée sur des prépuces
    sanguinolents
je n'ai que des ossements d'il y a mille ans que je ramasse
que j'entasse

once the glory of our turbans and our heart at
    sword level
In your opacity you are a mirror
you know our blood as famous from its rotten journeys
you know us as a wonder in a desert of blindness
our females such regenerators of white
    citadels
where when I was a poet
on behalf of my blood spilled on a stone
I too proclaimed a doe grazing beneath the palm tree
    a goddess

You know our catastrophe our distress our
    countries in outright earthquake
earthquake of the brow and earthquake of the gaze beckoning
    the shipwreck
you know which ruins and which dreads make
    our eyes beautiful
you know our prophylactics against the gambling streets
our fratricidal impasses when on reckoning day
we buy at auction any genealogy that will lift sequestration

You know from which imperious earth and which empty tomb
we quarry our wanderings our menacing ages our Doubt
and this childhood
full of young dogs razor-cut to know
us as shut-ins at death's door
You know and I will not spread jasmine in the streets
I will not build a mausoleum on bloody
    foreskins
I have only thousand-year-old bones that I gather
that I hoard

sur le chemin des exils et vous attends
et depuis que j'attends il n'y a pas une seule nuit
qui eût été capitale dans l'espoir
sauf quand c'est la pénombre-même
qui doit assassiner mon ombre

Depuis les nuits passent les squelettes restent
depuis que nous sommes nuits à balafres et depuis
    les cimetières à vif
déracinant l'aube dans nos voix mendiantes
depuis que nous sommes dans cette nuit de couteau
déchirant la soie du désir
dans cette chair aux aguets l'équivalent d'un attentat public
sur la voie des rêves
depuis que nous sommes par centaines de fourmis
    rampant à émietter le souvenir
riches en signes de désastre que de porte en porte
    vous les nuits de palingénésie
vous transformez en prophétie irradiante
depuis l'art l'agonie les coups d'état la beauté les soulèvements
de la mémoire
depuis l'éléphant qui porte le messager du destin transitant
par le rire de qui a eu le malheur de devenir fou
depuis Shahrayar dans ses flaques de sperme et de sang
depuis la mort depuis le vin depuis notre impossibilité d'être
autrement qu'en nous sentant arrachés à nous-mêmes
    déhanchés dans le gouffre
depuis toujours
il n'y a pas une seule nuit qui ne m'eût conté la fable
du poisson vert déguisé en miracle à hauteur de nos prunelles

on the path of exiles and I expect you
and since I've been expecting not one single night
has been central to my hope
except when it's the dusk itself
that must assassinate my shadow

Since the nights pass the skeletons remain
since we became scarred nights and since
    the living cemeteries
uprooting the dawn in our beggar voices
since we are in this knife night
ripping the silk of desire
in this alert flesh the equivalent of a public ambush
on the path of dreams
since the hundreds of ants
    climbing to indebt memory
made us rich in signs of disaster that from door to door
    you the nights of palingenesis
you transform into shining prophesy
since art agony coups d'état beauty uprisings
of memory
since the elephant carrying destiny's messenger passing through
the laughter of whoever had the misfortune of going crazy
since Shahryar in his puddles of sperm and blood
since death since wine since our impossibility of being
other than in feeling ripped from ourselves
    unhinged in the void
since forever
there's not a single night that hasn't told me the fable
of the green fish disguised as a miracle at eye level

Or mon attente à moi ne quémande pas de feu-follet à l'entour
n'est pas mule broutant un verbe captif des pierres noires
est un cri est l'incendie
des capitales qui dorment
est comme un soleil neuf
                    à l'est
                        à l'errance.

Yet my personal expectation doesn't go cap in hand for any will-
    o-the-wisp nearby
is not a mule grazing on a word held captive by black stones
is a cry is the conflagration
of slumbering capitals
is like a new sun
                in the east
                        wandering.

AL

SHAHRAZADE LA LANGUE

Je veux quand il fait nuit Shahrazade
que tu ne persistes plus avec ces étoiles
tu ne sais avec tes pierres miroitantes rien de ce
 voyage huitième
où il fait jour depuis qu'il ne fait pas jour
où il fait nuit pour toujours
où je me tais sous l'invasion de ma langue
par les buissons du refus d'une langue autre que la mienne
 par essence
absolument tout autre que la mienne pour sortir
 et guetter ton ombre
dire et répéter ton ombre
m'armer d'un poignard et guetter ton ombre
jouer avec la lune aux billes et guetter ton ombre
mon unique ombre dénombrée de moi du dedans
 aux pieds de ton ombre
un rêve perpétuel dans la bouche pour gonfler du
 papier-glacé et que je le claque
sur les portes de l'infini
l'absurdité de l'infini dans mon corps
assassiné
humilié
vampire

SCHEHERAZADE THE TONGUE

I want when it is night Scheherazade
for you to stop it with these stars
you with your sparkling rocks know nothing about this
    eighth voyage
where it's been daylight since daylight ended
where it is night forever
where I go quiet with the invasion of my tongue
by the thicket defying a tongue essentially
    other than mine
absolutely other than mine to go out
    and lie in wait for your shadow
to speak and repeat your shadow
to arm myself with a dagger and wait for your shadow
to play marbles with the moon and wait for your shadow
my single shadow measured by myself from the insides
    to the feet of your shadow
a perpetual dream in the mouth to inflate
    glazed paper and that I slam
against the doors of the infinite
the absurdity of the infinite in my body
assassinated
humiliated
vampire

Je ne veux plus d'étoiles
je veux une nuit belle parce que dénuée de signes
        et fermée à toute chose
je veux dans cette nuit apercevoir ton ombre et te servir un
        superbe gâteau
où l'étoileur dont tu lis l'avenir sanglote :
mes cuites mes mensonges ma nomadité chronique
        et ses cavernes
te servir une génisse enceinte de moi sur-place morte
de qui a l'œil humide où mille soleils pleurent comme
        oiseaux sans nom
tout à fait ce qu'il faut pour que tu manges et te détendes
        et que je te dise mange
mange de toute ton âme avec tes ongles tes tresses
        et tes miroirs
mange et dis-toi qu'il n'y a pas de place en nous pour la cité de
        cuivre aux écritures d'ombre
et que nous sommes liés à la cité de cuivre par
        stupéfaction du corps
par des voyages à mort
par vacuité de langue
par la mygale somptueuse de ton délire qui resplendit après la mort
par la solitude et par des dynasties entières à
        interpréter faciès et longueur du crâne
pacifiés, nous autres, par les arbres

Je veux quand il fait nuit Shahrazade que tu ne me proclames plus
ton époux de désespoir à cause de ma langue
à cause du bédouin qui intenta à ma langue l'abîme de sa langue
et enterra ma langue
à cause de la monture du bédouin qui enterra sa
        monture et enterra ma langue

I don't want any more stars
I want a night that is beautiful because devoid of signs
    and shut off from everything
I want in that night to perceive your shadow and serve you a
    superb cake
where the stargazer whose future you're reading sobs:
my drunken stupors my lies my chronic nomadism
    and its caverns
to serve you a heifer I impregnated killed on the spot
by the one with wet eyes where a thousand suns weep like
    nameless birds
exactly what is necessary for you to eat and relax
    and for me to tell you eat
eat with all your soul with your nails your hair
    and your mirrors
eat and tell yourself there's no place in us
    for the bronze society with its shadow-writing
and that we are linked to the bronze society by
    bodily amazement
by journeys to death
by the vacuity of tongues
by the sumptuous tarantula of your delirium resplendent after death
by solitude and whole dynasties to
    interpret features and skull length
calmed, the rest of us, by the trees

I want when it is night Scheherazade for you to stop declaring me
your husband of despair because of my tongue
because of the bedouin who took action against my tongue the abyss
    of his tongue
and buried mine
because of the mount of the bedouin who buried his
    mount and buried my tongue

et me laissa mortellement à plat ventre avec la certitude qu'un jour
je ferai corps avec les algues
et à même ton ombre n'existant que par le seul
        manège de mon chant lié
vêtu de mon seul corps exsangue dans la nuit noire
sans récitation dans ma fugue
tant que tes pieds n'auront pas foulé la mer et n'auront pas été
là où toutes les boussoles craquent de tous les enfers de ma langue
où j'existe tu n'existes que par suppression de racines
que par enchantement de ma main qui sait la caresse
        des vieilles pierres
et me souhaite
la mort par fixation de décombres
je ne sais où te mettre je m'esquive je ne fais que je

je suis à vrai dire sans peuple sans patrie sans aucune référence
à ce que j'oublie
à vrai dire sans aucune voix
de rempart
dans la nuit où je ne puis entrer
à vrai dire sans écriture sans livre sans préceptes ni prophétie
avec de l'air vert dans mes vallées
de l'air vert sur des places endormies pour piéger l'attente
mon désespoir adulte
les statues étranglées par leur propre musique comme
        sirènes de pacotille
qui n'ont pas de rives et n'ont pas d'âge
je ne sais où te mettre
ni comment oublier et mourir

ni comment oublier et me taire et perdre ma langue
        quand il fait nuit
et que tu apparais et que c'est vers toi que je regarde

and left me mortally flat on the floor with the certainty that one day
I would be one with the seaweed
and even your shadow existing solely because of the lone
    carousel of my linked song
dressed in my lone body bloodless in the dark night
with no recitation in my fugue
as long as your feet haven't trodden the sea and haven't been
there where all compasses crack with all the infernos of my tongue
where I exist you only exist by suppressing roots
by enchanting my hand which knows the caress
    of old stones
and wishing me
death by rubble fixation
I don't know where to put you I dodge I only I

I am honestly without people without country without any reference
to what I forget
honestly without any defensive
voice
in the night where I cannot enter
honestly without writing without book without precepts or prophesy
with green air in my valleys
green air on sleeping plazas to trap the expectation
my adult despair
statues strangled by their own music like
    dime-store sirens
with no shores and no age
I don't know where to put you
or how to forget and die

or how to forget and fall silent and lose my tongue
    when it is night
and you appear and I look towards you

et que ma nuit n'a pas lieu sur ces mêmes places
    où le désert a les dunes de demain
ni demain ni après-demain quand je serai porte-parole
    de la mort blanche
avec dix mille ans de solitude en brouillard fin
apprivoisé dans un flacon
ni le vautour savant qui me suit partout et qui parle
parce qu'il possède une langue et me procure femme
    et nourriture à tout moment
– nous aimer dans des grottes et puis va-t'en
pour que débarrassé enfin du temps de l'absent du
    ciel de la mer des arbres et de l'aride
je n'aime que toi et puis va-t'en
comme on s'aime dans l'écume noire
pour que le songe aie moins de cent ans et moins
    d'un jour et soit
plus bref que la fraction infinitésimale des mesures
    temporelles de l'angoisse
    afin que je possède une langue
    sans avoir souvenance de posséder une langue
afin que dans une soudaine irruption au milieu des corbeaux
ma langue provoque une envolée noire sans
    signification à l'intérieur de ma langue
afin que tes doigts quand ils reculent dans le temps
    me ramènent
les temps reculés dans une ville belle parmi toutes
    où reprendre
    l'émeute l'émeute l'émeute
    le retour en force de l'émeute
ton esprit devenu combinaison chimique et rien
    d'autre qu'un simple corps en convalescence
ton esprit dans ses coquilles dans ses prismes dans
    sa carapace de tortue

and my night does not take place on these same plazas
    where the desert keeps tomorrow's dunes
not tomorrow or the day after when I'm the voice
    of white death
with ten thousand years of solitude in fine fog
subdued in a flask
or the savant vulture who follows me everywhere and speaks
because it possesses a tongue and procures me woman
    and food every minute
– love us in caves and then get out
so that finally rid of time the absent the
    sky the sea trees and the arid
I love only you and then get out
like we love each other in the black foam
to make the daydream less than a hundred years old and less
    than a day old and
more brief than the infinitesimal fraction of temporal
    measures of anguish
    so that I possess a tongue
    without remembering I possess a tongue
so that in a sudden eruption in the middle of crows
my tongue provokes a black flight with no
    sense inside my tongue
so that your fingers when they go back in time
    bring me back
distant times in the fairest city of them all
    a place to take up again
    the riot the riot the riot
    the forceful return of the riot
your mind now a chemical combination and nothing
    besides a simple convalescing body
your mind in its shells in its prisms in
    its turtle shell

ton esprit dans la métaphore de sa source de graisseet de lymphe
qui tire vers le rose et le noir
la corrélation fuligineuse de ton cerveau son abîme
en crachat sur les dalles des vagues des feuilles d'automne
animalité fangeuse immonde quelconque de ton nez
    et de ton gosier fatal
oh je veux quand il fait nuit avoir dix mille doigts d'attente
qui s'ouvrent se referment
autour de ton cou et du cou d'isabelle ma maîtresse noire
intenter ma nuit dans le désert le vrai
dans l'anti-temps
où je m'agenouille fort de quelques tombeaux sâadiens
    vieillis de mémoire
ou à demi fou sur un cheval
sans avoir le sentiment de posséder une langue
qui me lave de toute hantise
et des ténèbres
                pour égorger toutes les autruches
de volupté et dans ma ténèbre éclater le roseau pensant
l'ogre la pègre de mon sang noir de poète qui vomit
et propre à la nuit et désespéré comme le soupir le
plus profond à trois jets de sperme de
moi-même écroulant le mont ararat pour n'aimer
que toi et puis va-t'en
    l'émeute si tu revenais
      le retour en force perpétuel et constant de l'émeute
    si je t'aimais
            dans la nuit terrorisée des conteurs
    en révolte

your mind in the metaphor of its source of fat and lymph
pulling toward the pink and black
the sooty correlation of your brain its abyss
as spittle on the slab-like waves of autumn leaves
some muddy squalid animality of your nose
    and your fatal craw
oh I want when it is night to have ten thousand expectant fingers
opening and closing
around your neck and that of isabelle my black mistress
take action my night in the desert the real one
in anti-time
where I kneel strong with several Saadian tombs
    aged by memory
or half-mad on a horse
without feeling I possess a tongue
that washes me clean of all obsessive fear
and of darkness
                to slit the throats of all the ostriches
of luxury and in my dark burst the reed thinking
the ogre the mob of my black blood a vomiting poet's
and belonging to the night and hopeless like the
deepest sigh with three spurts of sperm from
me collapsing mount ararat to love
only you and then get out
    the riot if you came back
    the forceful perpetual and constant return of the riot
    if I loved you
           in the terrorized night of the storytellers
    in revolt

AL

DÉSERT...

désert

mais c'est la disposition tombale de tes tentes, cette
    géométrie de sépulcres découpés dans l'immobilité du
    souvenir, voilà ce que je chante

tes vieilles tentes qui, dressées là où un jour de mes tourbillons a
    vagi ta température (comme toi j'ai des vents de tout âge) dé-
    signent l'emplacement exact de mon prénom, abritent l'origine
    de ma soif, fraient un passage à la poussée latente de mes désirs,
    dénotent l'un de ces paroxysmes de ma tribu qui, en sauvegar-
    dant l'emblème de son écriture, entretient la cendre d'une pre-
    mière rencontre restée dans la bouche avec un goût de datte dont
    l'attente était le noyau ;

tes vieilles tentes si difficiles à situer dans la prophétie par la seule
    vertu de l'index et l'état des écorchures au fond des poitrines

mais c'est du corps ancien en déroute que je te chante

prémices à l'émergence d'un continent entier aux rivages d'interro-
    gations ;

que ce soit dans les plus hautes tours fouettées de détritus, que la
    démence

m'y fasse ciseler l'onyx de nouvelles absences (la nuit-mère dans le
    vert-père)

ou que ma jouissance ailleurs fissure l'oubli et que je sois sans yeux,

c'est toujours moi, avec mes loques, qui suis ton Moïse qui suis ton
    cyclope,

qui suis tes dormeurs de la caverne puis l'écho de leurs voix,

qui suis celui

desert
but it's the tomb-like layout of your tents, that
    geometry of jagged sepulchers in the memory's
    stillness, that's what I sing
your old tents that erected where one of my whirlwind days your tem-
    perature wailed (like you I have winds of all ages), designate the
    exact placement of my first name, shelter the origin of my thirst,
    clear a passage to the latent thrust of my desires, denote one of
    my tribe's paroxysms that in saving the emblem of its writing
    maintains the ash of a first meeting that remained in the mouth
    tasting of dates expecting the the pit;
your old tents so difficult to place in the
    prophecy solely by virtue of the forefinger and state of
    scrapes deep inside chests
but I sing to you of the ancient body in full rout
presage of a whole continent's emergence on the shores of interroga-
    tion;
may it be in the highest towers whipped by refuse, may dementia
make me carve the onyx of new absences (the night-mother in the
    green-father)
or may my pleasure elsewhere fissure forgetfulness and may I be eye-
    less,
I, with my rags, am always your Moses your cyclops,
your sleepers of the cave then the echo of their voices,
the one

apostrophant le scorpion maître du suicide pour l'apprivoiser m'y
    insinuer m'égarer mourir et m'extasier d'une figue de barbarie
    dans cette errance,
qui suis ta fable et ton prométhée qui suis ta langue
    et l'histoire la plus opaque dans ton eau la plus
    glauque qui suis ton menhir en matière éclatante,
l'île qui est l'homme
dénué de toute parenté
épuisant toutes les négations ;
qui dis à ma détresse mais reste ne pars pas car si tu pars
entre les doigts crochus d'un espoir à la renverse ne laisseras que
    quelques cheveux que quelques bribes de présence
comme des loques aux devantures de mes villes de mort ;
qui ne puis écrire de lettre ni de télégramme sans énoncer
une protestation à morsures à l'adresse de dieu et de ses anges
et ne peux allumer de feu nocturne qui brûle à vif l'oiseau de folie et
    d'enfance près de ma mémoire sans
que tout mon dedans ne soit le gage d'une future saignée à l'intérieur
    de ma tête
tout mon dedans formé de nappes de pus et de sang s'annonce un
    royaume noir où des mendiants exorcisent le réel, chaque jour
    dans le silence de la pierre
dans la chair crue de tes vents une mer unique, engloutie dans le
    corps et qui s'avance
vers des horizons qui hurlent, voilà la réalité de mon attente.

apostrophizing the scorpion adept at suicide to tame it get in its
    good graces stray die and wax poetic for a prickly pear in this
    wandering,
I am your fable and your prometheus am your tongue
    and the most opaque story in your murkiest
    water am your menhir clothed in dazzling material,
the island who is man
devoid of all relations
exhausting all the negations;
I say to my distress but stay don't leave because if you leave
between the claw-like fingers of a backwards hope you'll leave nothing
    behind but a few hairs a few scraps of presence
like rags in the storefronts of my cities of death;
I can write neither letter nor telegram without protesting
in soundbites to god and this angels
and cannot light a night fire to burn the bird of madness and child-
    hood alive near my memory without
all my guts being the forfeit for a future bled dry inside my head
all my guts formed of layers of pus and blood a black kingdom de-
    clares itself where beggars exorcise the real, every day in the si-
    lence of stone
in the raw flesh of your winds a single sea, engulfed in the body and
    advancing
toward screaming horizons, such is the reality of my expectation.

AL

ANTICIPATION SUR UNE EXCLUSION

Moi nomade
je guéris par écritures de sable
les plaies du devenir dans l'attente
je traquerai l'image de la mort
    en vous
vos chemins d'étoiles et là où elle sera présente
avec des caftans des bouquets de kif
parrainant les mirages la mort
très belle comme la lecture souveraine de nos mains

Parce que je nous Vois
je cracherai mes souvenirs au petit jour
    sans vous
mes parentés inaudibles dans des eaux troubles de
    matins incertains
je serai celui
dont la voix est native de villes jetées à leurs défaites
en débris de ciel qui les hante
qui ne connais pas mon nom mon origine je serai
le moi-sang
pour ne plus jamais rêver.

La mort est toute rouge qui découvre
son hibou flamboyant et la matité d'une lune endormie
dans les sources

ANTICIPATION OF AN EXCLUSION

I nomad
I heal through sand writings
the wounds of becoming in waiting
I'll track the image of death
    in you
your star paths and there where it will be present
with kaftans with kif bouquets
fostering mirages death
very beautiful like the sovereign reading of our hands

Because I See us
I'll spit out my remembrances at dawn
    without you
my inaudible kinships in the troubled waters of
    uncertain early mornings
I'll be the one
whose voice is native to cities thrown to their defeats
in debris of heavens that haunt them
who does not know my name my origin I'll be
the blood-me
so as never again to dream.

Death is red all-over who discovers
its blazing owl and the dullness of a moon asleep
in its sources

Mémoire maudite

Dès lors je parle la langue héritée d'une grande nuit répandue

Moi nomade
je voudrais comme dans un rite ancien et porteur d'un masque
je voudrais avec des terrains mouvants
je voudrais avec des cycles de corps emmurés dans
    la boue je voudrais
d'hier à demain
avec des rues piégées d'hommes sans yeux comme
    des soleils éteints
avec des rues sans ville avec des villes sans nom je voudrais
comme un poisson arriver par les coutumes d'eau qui
    ponctuent ton nom d'une île dans mon regard
je voudrais comme un nuage intense sur des moissons sans terre
comme une possibilité de vie autre comme un cri
revenir
et infliger à ton corps le spectacle de mes péninsules d'ombre
trancher notre difficulté d'être
ou mourir
Je parle
la moitié de ma langue où le soleil est une fissure
tandis que dans l'autre moitié tout entre nous reste mille fois
à redire
le soleil est dans ma langue
le gemme phosphorescent résumant des nuits vénéneuses
et de porphyre en toi
préservant à jamais de ma venue
les brumes de tes rives et la terre ferme de tes contes à ogives
le soleil dans ma pomme d'Adam

Memory damned

From here on I speak the language inherited from a vast spread
    out night

I nomad
I would like as in an ancient rite and wearing a mask
I would like with moving grounds
I would like with cycles of bodies walled
    in the mud I'd like
from yesterday to tomorrow
with streets boobytrapped with men with eyes like
    extinct suns
with streets without cities with cities without names I would like
to arrive like a fish according to the customs of water that
    punctuate your name with an island in my gaze
I would like like an intense cloud over crops
    without soil
like a life possibility that is other like a cry
to come back
and inflict on your body the spectacle of my shadow peninsulas
cut through our difficulty of being
or die
I speak
that half of my language where the sun is a fissure
while in the other half everything between us remains a thousand
    times
to be resaid
the sun is in my language
the phosphorescent jewel summing up venomous nights
of porphyry inside you
protecting forever from my sight
the fogs of your shores and the solid earth of your warheaded tales
the sun in my Adam's apple

éclate les digues du refus sur la mer que je bois entièrement
  pour t'entendre je voudrais lire
sur tes seins l'alphabet rose
des solitudes de la peine et les prédictions de toutes les mon-
tagnes à venir

Nomade
pour ruiner une religion par jour sans me départir de moi-même
c'est-à-dire du fracas et des éruptions de plutonium de mon
sang veillant sur les remparts
  des palais de jade
  des mausolées de nacre
je voudrais ruiner une religion par jour et tous les temples d'or
dans mes souvenirs – tendre des pièges aux fantômes
qui se risquent hors de l'oubli
J'arrive
par la caravane
sortie de la grande déchirure
de l'espace.

bursts the dams of refusal on the sea that I drink all up
    to hear you I would like to read
on your breasts the pink alphabet
of pain's solitudes and the predictions of all the mountains
    to come

Nomad
to ruin one religion a day without straying from myself
that is from the fracas and plutonium eruptions of my blood
standing watch on the ramparts
    of the jade palaces
    of the mother-of-pearl mausoleums
I would like to ruin one religion a day and all the golden temples
in my memories – set traps for the phantoms
that venture out of forgetting
I arrive
by the caravan
come out of the great gash
in space.

comme qui a déclaré son amour à l'araignée et s'en est allé
parti lavé de toute chose boudant tous les arbres
je périrai
en aparté
criant ma durée
devant une ville désertée

comme qui a rejeté père et mère pour n'adopter que la figure de
sa propre absence
— gestes en forêts
depuis
les meurtrières
des villes-mirages
l'interrogation essentielle de mon corps définitif
est un palmier dattier
dans la nuit des nausées
mes rêves
sur des chemins de roses fanées
citadelles à hauteur de l'exil mes dires
royaumes de silence
édifiés sur l'ignorance de la lecture
je me suis embusqué
pour parler leur agonie
pour parler du temps et des pensées insolites du temps
et des voyages accomplis par la langue les sens
repensant la réalité et les habitudes
de mon corps mille fois exclu
un jour je reviendrai

like he who declared his love to the spider and walked out
left everything washed off disdaining all the trees
I'll perish
as an aside
screaming my duration
before a deserted city

like one who has rejected mother and father so as to adopt
only the figure of his own absence
– gestures in forests
from
the embrasures
of the mirage-cities
the essential interrogation of my definitive body
is a date palm
in the night of nauseas
my dreams
on paths of faded roses
citadels at the height of exile my sayings
realms of silence
erected on the ignorance of reading
I'm waiting in ambush
to speak their agony
to speak of time and of time's bizarre thoughts
and of the journeys undertaken by language by the senses
rethinking the real and the habits
of my body a thousand times excluded
some day I'll return

pour dire la phrase en ruine des cloportes et des damnés
et des silhouettes à abattre
dans des aéroports dévastés
un jour je reviendrai
je serai foule à décrire ma mort postérieure à l'apocryphe
l'espace désolé de mes sangs désertiques
le néant le départ l'écriture l'alphabet et l'oubli
n'auront ainsi jamais existé
un jour
le scorpion mystique chevauchera la nuit
et l'escargot sera ce maître du désert qui le poursuit
un jour de folie un jour de violence
je reviendrai détaché de ma pensée
la seule qui me restera de la mille et deuxième nuit

to speak the ruined sentence of the woodlice and the damned
and of the silhouettes to be cut down
in devastated airports
some day I'll return
I'll be crowd to describe my death posterior to the apocryphal
the desolate space of my arid bloods
nothingness the departure the writing the alphabet and forgetting
will thus never have existed
one day
the mystic scorpion will ride the night
and the snail will be that desert master that pursues it
on a day of madness a day of violence
I'll return detached from my thought
the only one left me of the thousand and second night

du rocher noir de tous les réels et le scinque me léguant sa raison
ville
j'endosse à ta vue le cadavre puant d'une bête errante et je
    déchire mon nom
l'aveugle ferré à son angoisse prie mais moi j'éclate les limbes
du jour et mon œil rétrécit
je ne te connais plus
        ville sans nom
je n'ai point mendié en toi ni les rêves de la colombe ni ceux
    de la tortue
je ne réalise même pas, fermant les yeux, me tâtant
comme tu as pu surgir avec des portes noires et si près
du bleu pur de ma haine savante
et avec autant d'anneaux en métal de nuit
je n'ai perdu en toi ni
mon profil ni les bijoux
    anciens de ma femme d'encre
ni rompu mes liens avec le passé du couteau
ville sans pierre sans émail sans architecte sûr
ni tracé tes rues avec mon imagination ni élevé le phoque
dans ton giron de flaque de marécage sec
                                ville blessure
au point de sentir mon corps échoué sans rêve sans pensée
sous une cité sans murs sous un sahara
mon corps lentement qui s'énonce
dans l'absence de l'eau et que je ne peux rapatrier
que si toute ma méditation éclate
que si ma méditation reprend sa forme d'explosion d'espace de
    feu

of the black rock of all the reals and the skink bequeathing me its mind
city
in sight of you I'll endorse the stinking corpse of an errant beast
        and I'll tear up my name
the blind man hobnailed to his anguish prays but I explode day's
limbo and my eye narrows
I no longer know you
        city without a name
in you I did not beg either for the dove's dreams
        nor for those of the tortoise
and closing my eyes and checking myself I can't even conceive
how you were able to surface suddenlywith black doors and so close
to the pure blue of my savant hate
and with so many rings of night metal
I lost in you neither
my profile nor the ancient
        jewelry of my ink woman
no did I cut my bonds with the past of the knife
city without stone without enamel without assured architect
nor traced your streets with my imagination nor raised the seal
in the midst of your dry swamp puddle
                              wound-city
to the point of feeling my body run aground dreamless thoughtless
beneath a wallless city beneath a sahara
my body which slowly enunciates itself
in the absence of water and that I can repatriate
only if the whole of my meditation explodes
only if my meditation again takes the its form of an explosion of
        a space of fire

et de révolution pour te dénommer : ville sans ville

tu as revêtu les apparats de la lune pour te convertir

en soleil et définitivement consacrer notre obsession d'un changement qui se résume dans le geste de la main renversée, mais on ne guérit pas si facilement des morsures de la nuit et moi je n'ai pas à t'offrir de diamants tirés des frimas ou des tropiques de mes cris, à ajouter des voies d'aube pour les seules échappées du sirocco mien, à mordre dans ton absence, et à offrir des joies de papyrus en animaux étranges refoulés dans des souvenirs

je me passe de toute ma vie d'un trait pour ne plus jamais en parler

ville du manège de l'iris impropre

autant que le permette le reptile prophète qui nous écoute et la libellule

je ne pense moi qu'à la ville qui ne se soulève plus qui a enraciné son ombre dans l'immobilité

à qui les âges ont fait des icebergs dans le cerveau et des poux secs sur toute la peau

je ne pense moi qu'à la mer lasse au rivage de ta préhistoire

à tout ce qui nous enchaîne en nous regardant

tout ce qui nous enfonce encore plus dans l'illusion des statues

nous qui déjà ne sommes plus que poupées de cendre

sous la mêlée des étoiles/ la folie noire/ le fracas et les oiseaux

and of a revolution to name you: cityless city
you have put on the stately attire of the moon to convert
yourself into a sun and to finally consecrate our obsession
for a change summed up in the gesture of your turned over
hand, but one doesn't heal so easily from night's bites and
I I don't have to offer you diamonds culled from the freez-
ing fogs or the tropics of my screams, to add dawn pas-
sageways for the sole escapes from my sirocco, to bite into
your absence, and to offer papyrus joys in strange animals
repressed into memories
I'll do without my life in one fell swoop never to talk of it again
city of the improper iris' goings-on
as far as permitted by the reptile prophet listening to us and
the dragonfly
me I think only of the city that doesn't rise up any longer that
has rooted its shadow in immobility
as the ages have made icebergs in its brain while
dry lice crawl all over its skin
me I think only of the tired sea at the shore of your prehistory
of everything that enchains us while looking at each other
everything that sinks us more deeply into the illusion of the statues
we who already are no more than dolls of ashes
below the stars' fray / black madness / the fracas and the birds

je périrai
en aparté
criant ma durée
devant une ville désertée

comme qui a déterminé le climat de ses racines
dans la profondeur du malaise
et de la boue
qui a dicté la phrase jugulée océane
et craché la moelle de l'éternité
qui a déclaré le démantèlement des réseaux de fascination
d'ici et d'ailleurs
par rapport à son malaise
qui s'est mué en tonnerre changeant
et n'a plus réapparu (moi)

je
est déjà mort en conjuguant
des après-midis sans prière
en forçant dans la mémoire des hantises de pierre ponce
mort avec un énorme caméléon pour comploter contre les nues
et porteur d'étendues verdoyantes
qui sont toutes à la mesure
des négations
bien mort
sans papiers sans victuailles sans argent sans demeure
très loin dans la sieste du bidonville

I'll perish
as an aside
screaming my duration
before a deserted city

like he who has defined the climate of his roots
in the depths of unease
and mud
who has dictated the throttled oceanic sentence
and spat out the marrow of eternity
who has declared the dismantling of the networks of fascination
of here and elsewhere
in relation to his unease
which has mutated into thunder changing
and hasn't reappeared (me)

I
is already dead while conjugating
afternoons without prayers
while forcing pumice-stone hauntings into memory
dead with an enormous chameleon for conspiring against the clouds
and carrier of vast verdant spaces
that are all commensurate
with the negations
dead indeed
without papers without victuals without money without dwelling
deep inside the ghetto's siesta

et croyant franchement que je puis être Dieu
à titre définitif
dans Babylone
que j'aurais moi-même peinte en bleu

exclu mort me reprenant
parce que je ne sais pas écrire mon désir
ni son histoire faite de complots ni en décrire
le ciel bas devant mes yeux
je ne sais pas dire les proportions alarmantes de mon désir
devant toi ville en butte à mon corps brisé
ville toute blanche sur la terre de yahah yahah
où mon sang chante l'amnésie du taureau – je ne sais pas écrire
    mon désir
qui a le mauvais goût de broyer mon regard
et qu'il écrabouille comme font les nymphomanes du lièvre torride
sur les routes de dépression
je ne sais pas fomenter ou libérer mon désir
sans le sentiment que tout s'effondre et que la terre s'ouvre
dans ma première langue-être
– le cauchemar du désert insinué
dans les plis de la rose des vents –
la rue qui a vu naître et mourir mon désir
dans les coulées immondices et férocités
où je suis la foule identique à soi-même dans l'espace renouvelé

and frankly believing that I can be God
definitively
in Babylon
which I'd have painted blue

excluded death taking me back
because I do not know how to write my desire
nor its history made of conspiracies nor how to describe
the low sky before my eyes
I do not know how to say the alarming proportions of my desire
before you city exposed to my broken body
all white city on the earth of yahah yahah
where my blood sings the bull's amnesia – I don't know how to
    write my desire
that has the bad taste to crush my gaze
and that it smashes as do the nymphomaniacs with the torrid hare
on depression road
I do not know how to foment or liberate my desire
without feeling that everything collapses and that the earth opens
in my first language-being
– the nightmare of the desert insinuated
into the folds of the wind-rose –
the street that has seen my desire being born and die
in the mudslide of refuse and ferocities
where I am the crowd identical with itself in the rekindled space

4

je périrai, en aparté, plein le cœur d'un ciel de cyanure
mais seulement après avoir été à la grotte de l'écrit brûlant
pour capter toute ma mémoire intacte
la chambre aux mille caractères
où s'achève le périple de ma soif

et j'y reste – défendant qu'on me pose
des questions sur la façon dont j'y reste
sur l'état de ma raison
sur l'identité de mon cri
dans les demeures de la nuit

sur la mort qui est une avancée d'impasses
soulevées par le soleil
sur les étendues de violence renaissant
chaque jour dans le silence
de ma langue gercée.

4

I'll perish, as an aside, heart filled with a cyanide sky
but only after having been to the cave of burning writing
to capture my memory whole and intact
the room of a thousand characters
where the periplos of my thirst ends

and I stay there – not allowing
questions on the manner of my staying there
on the state of my reason
on the identity of my scream
in night's dwellings

on death which is a headway of dead-ends
raised up by the sun
on the vast spaces of renaissant violence
each day in the silence
of my cracked tongue.

PJ

DIURNE

Mort je bois ton eau pour me savoir séparé de moi-même
séparé de ma dernière langue et tu mutiles ma langue
séparé comme si d'un geste consacrant la déchirure
et la fin des serments d'encre
je me souvenais d'une absence ô combien claire
antérieure au refus précédant même le je négateur

précédant les possibles mutations et une consécration
de larmes dans mes privilèges sur les cailloux et les plantes
par ce cri autrefois lancé dans un désert

j'ai vécu natif d'un puits perdu dans le regard des origines
ses cruautés peintes à vif sur mes guenilles j'ai vécu
l'incursion de tes paysages le cumul de leurs gouffres
tes sables et tes danses
tes rêves et tous les synonymes dans la marche
du bousier tourmenté par l'azur dans ses pièges à squelettes
L'invisible
est comme une réalité fixe par-delà les survivances du poème

Je sais ma raison sous la glace
qui provoque une extension de terres sans nom
c'est une mouvance
de plateaux dans ma poitrine qui reculent en geignant
chaque jour rend plus vivace
en moi l'inaccoutumance des oasis au désert des extases
d'où je renie les remparts mauves dans l'éternité de leur boue

DIURNAL

Dead I drink your water to know I'm separated from myself
separated from my last tongue and you mutilate my tongue
separated as though with a gesture consecrating the rip
and the end of ink oaths
I remembered an absence oh how clear
before the refusal that preceded even the denying I

preceded the possible mutations and a consecration
of tears in my privileges on the pebbles and plants
by that cry once launched in a desert

I lived as a native of a well lost in the eyes of origins
its cruelties painted raw on my rags I lived
the invasion of your landscapes the build-up of their voids
your sands and your dances
your dreams and all the synonyms in the steps
of the dung beetle tormented by the blue in his skeleton traps
The invisible
is like a fixed reality on the other side of the poem's relics

I know my reason under the ice
that provokes an extension of unnamed earths
it's a shifting
of plateaus in my chest that retreat groaning
every day makes the estrangement
from oases in the desert of ecstasies stronger in me
thus I renounce the mauve ramparts in their eternal mud

ô ma raison sous le sabot de qui je fus qui te piétine
d'une syllabe tu inventes des ressacs dans la mêlée des ombres
puis des montagnes puis des lacs et enfin le poisson-sang à renaître
du séisme de mon moi extrayant l'angoisse
de vieilles villes tôt supposées belles à l'entrée de mes grottes

oh my reason under the hoof of who I was that tramples you
from a syllable you invent eddies in the free-for-all of shadows
then from the mountains then the lakes and finally the fish-blood
    to be born again
from the earthquake of my self extracting the anguish
of old cities first thought beautiful at the entrance of my caves

AL

Approche du désertique

APPROACH TO THE DESERT SPACE

1997

❖

Translated by Guy Bennett

I

Ton pays quand il surnage
dans des syllabes orphelines
ce pays-là est acquis à un patrimoine d'absence
tant il est insaisissable entre deux rêveries
il s'enveloppe parfois des réverbérations de la plaine
et il y a un cyprès sur la pente d'une colline
pour s'appliquer à l'équilibre de l'horizon
et pour que tout autour le temps
puisse rester à jamais immobile

Mais toi au milieu
debout dans l'affinité des tombeaux
c'est comme si tu étais encore
le même voyageur anonyme
le voyageur que tu dis longtemps préparé
à la gravité de l'observation des dunes
celui qui a une ombre comme revisitée
dans sa trame profonde
ses prolongements essentiels
et qui a vu de cette structure ambivalente
de cette perspective en fragmentation
de ce champ d'inconnaissance
s'engager la latitude vagabonde
l'instance du désertique où le corps
ne peut plus revendiquer d'appartenance

Your country when it lingers on
in orphaned syllables
that country now belongs to a patrimony of absence
so elusive is it between musings
it is veiled at times by echoes from the plain
and a cypress stands on the slope of a hill
to keep the horizon in balance
and so that all around time
may be forever still

But you in the middle
standing in an affinity of tombs
you still seem
the same anonymous traveler
the traveler long ready you claim
for the solemn observation of dunes
the one with a shadow seemingly revisited
in its profound texture
its essential elongations
and which has seen the restless latitude
the entreaties of the desert space where the body
can no longer demand belonging
begin with this ambivalent structure
this fragmented perspective
this field of unknowing

D'autres ont une ombre sur la terre
en analogie avec matière lumière et espace
sans se poursuivre jusqu'aux frontières
de toutes les dissemblances

Alors te vient le désir de circonscrire ici même
l'ultime métaphore dans des paroles qui amalgament
confusément la position des astres
avec les points d'achoppement des dénégations
qui situent approximativement l'axe
réservé à l'occultation de sa propre matière
sous un ciel demeuré relié à un désordre tellurique
où chaque lieu a conservé
une lune immuable incorporée
comme incrustation souveraine
pour une métrique ineffable du désert

métaphore à partir du conifère et du laurier rose
pour qu'ils figurent ensemble
le portique réservé à l'examen des étoiles
à partir des arbres produisant du côté des ramures
une irruption de souvenance
jusqu'à doter la mémoire à chaque étape
d'une conformité avec l'exubérance des dunes
avec les serments de jadis les aveux d'expiation
mêlés à une attente de prodige
une communion incessante entre des carnets d'errance
et incidemment une surrection de calligraphies immarcescibles
perpétuant par leur romance
comme une rhétorique du désir
dissimulée derrière des touffes de marrube

Others cast a shadow on the earth
in analogy with matter light and space
without being pursued to the limits
of all dissimilarities

Then you are seized by the desire to define on this very spot
the ultimate metaphor in words that amalgamate
vaguely the position of the stars
with the stumbling blocks of denials
that give the approximate logistics of the axis
reserved for the occultation of its own matter
under a sky still linked to a telluric disorder
in which each place has preserved
an unchanging moon incorporated
as supreme incrustation
for an ineffable metrics of the desert

metaphor from the conifer and laurel rose
that together they may represent
the portico reserved for the study of stars
from the trees producing on the bough side
an irruption of recollection
to the point of granting memory at every step
a consonance with the exuberance of dunes
with the sermons of old the confessions of atonement
mixed with an expectation of miracles
an incessant communion between notebooks of wandering
and incidentally a surrection of imperishable calligraphies
perpetuating through their romance
a seeming rhetoric of desire
hidden behind tufts of horehound

une métaphore qui équivaut à oublier
tout à la fois les palmiers
que leur majesté presque désespérée
en silhouettes inclinées sur des cartes imaginaires
ainsi que la ville au milieu qui affecte aux nuages
l'incarnation légère de ses sépultures
qui déploie au-dessus de minarets rouges et mauves
un itinéraire perpétuel de cigognes
une ville où tant de fois on aurait voulu
dormir mourir puis ressusciter avant d'en repartir
car alors qu'il ne restait plus entre les lèvres
que l'interrogation itinérante de la pierre
une femme à l'aube venait retirer le suaire
préparait avec des résidus d'encres
l'électuaire qui délivre
de l'introversion des clepsydres

et la mer entière s'égarait au-dedans au-dehors
dans l'immensité du corps et les canyons de son cri
avec ces cargaisons d'alphabet neutralisé
qui acclimatent l'enfance en l'envahissant
d'origines toutes préméditées

une mer où des navires qui profilent des coques
toute reluisantes du sang coupé des sirènes
font le lien entre le sommeil et l'éveil
sans qu'on sache jamais s'ils se dirigent vers le rivage
ou si c'est le rivage qui cherche à les atteindre

a metaphor equivalent to forgetting
both the palm trees
and their almost desperate majesty
in silhouettes bent over imaginary maps
as well as the city in the middle which assigns to the clouds
the light incarnation of its sepulchers
unfurling over red and mauve minarets
a perpetual route of storks
a city where so often we would have liked
to sleep die then come back to life before setting out again
for then nothing remained between the lips
but the itinerant interrogation of stone
a woman at dawn was coming to remove the shroud
was preparing with inky residues
the electuary that releases us
from the introversion of clepsydræ

and the entire sea lost its way within without
in the immensity of the body and the canyons of its cry
with its cargoes of neutralized alphabet
which acclimate childhood by engulfing it
with wholly premeditated origins

a sea where ships sketching out hulls
glistening over with the blood cut from sirens
sail back and forth between sleep and waking
without our ever knowing whether they are heading for shore
or whether the shore is trying to reach them

comme une coïncidence d'écume avec un pays
qui ne cesse de se rejoindre
de se perdre se réamorcer et à nouveau se perdre
inscrit chaque fois dans une finalité décisive avant
d'être dévolu aux mots qui n'ont pas été dits
aux fragments de mots encore embués de leur silence
à la glose du sédiment même dans des livres
reliés de songes de peau et d'azur aux constellations éteintes

like a coincidence of foam with a country
that never stops catching up with itself
getting lost starting over and getting lost again
inscribed each time in a decisive finality before
being devolved into words unsaid
into fragments of words still misted over with their silence
into the gloss of sediment even in books
bound in dreams skin and blue with extinguished constellations

Le voyage où se réinventent
les topographies désertées de leur sud
c'est d'abord
une étendue inachevée

la présence attenante
aux régions hypothétiques
d'une identité échappée
près de se répandre
maintenant
dans une nouvelle interrogation redressée

c'est l'exégèse à blanc
qui m'incombe toute et la cendre
à partir d'un ciel vu qui recule
dans les épaisseurs du pseudonyme

le rivage qui s'établit
d'ici au mnémonique
quand la lune
a un éclat terni
d'ossements oraculaires
que sous la lune
des statues ont l'eau jusqu'au genou
pour parodier les temps de pénurie d'anges

The journey wherein topographies
deserted by their south are reinvented
is at first
an unfinished stretch of land

the presence adjoining
hypothetical regions
of a runaway identity
on the verge of spilling out
now
into a new rectified interrogation

it is the blank exegesis
which falls wholly to me and the ash
from an observed sky withdrawing
into the depths of pseudonymity

the shore that is established
from here to the mnemonic
when the moon
glows with the dull light
of oracular bones
that under the moon
statues stand knee-deep in water
to parody periods of angel shortages

et sous la précarité des nues
toute la contrainte du paysage
tel qu'il échut
au premier envol
du matin suspendu

and under the precariousness of clouds
the entire constraint of the landscape
such as it fell
at the first flight
of suspended morning

3

Voici un autre ciel
prééminence de l'ailleurs
sur les cheminements du vocable
comme résorption de l'azur
qui a servi d'ancrage
au corps antérieur

comme instant de haute rupture
qui réinvente une langue et la place hors d'atteinte
face à un point de simulation dans la plaine
de funérailles obscures
face à un réseau de ruelles
tentées dans une échancrure de réel
face à la primauté du possible et du probable
sur des confins imaginaires
il se refléta un jour dans mon âme
absorbant sa texture
avant une ultime dissociation en nuages

un autre ciel
avec toutes ces heures
à cristalliser dans l'abdomen
chargées des derniers flux
d'un potentiel d'hiéroglyphe
plus tard à communiquer
aux nuances du sel gemme

Here is another sky
preeminence of the elsewhere
along the progressions of the term
as reabsorption of the azure
which served as moorings
to the pre-body

like a moment of high rupture
that reinvents a language and places it out of reach
facing a point of simulation on the plain
of obscure funerals
facing a network of back alleys
attempted in an interstice of the real
facing the primacy of the possible and the probable
along imaginary borders
it was reflected one day in my soul
absorbing its texture
before a final separation into clouds

another sky
with all of these hours
to crystallize in the abdomen
loaded with the final fluxes
of hieroglyphic potential
later to communicate
with the nuances of rock salt

avec ce qui reste
constamment traversé
du repli de cette matière somnambule
parce qu'elle situe le pays perdu
à l'embouchure des songes
ses irruptions de jujubiers
sa persistance mordorée
d'éternité
dans une illumination fragmentaire

avec cette absence
arrivée à son seuil d'hyperbole
qui engage l'ombre sur un sol
que lui délimitent à son insu
pierres chaulées et spergules
où s'enclave à peine
une éclaircie supposée
presque le lieu où se concevoir
sans demeure sans mémoire
sans l'évocation d'un retour possible même
dans un temps autre
sa nuit hissée en catafalque
sur des épaules dénudées
pour enfin accéder
à la récitation qui alterne
étoiles et soleils se glaçant
dans cet écrit même
où cette cosmicité est tue

with what remains
constantly crossed
by the fold of this somnambulistic matter
because it situates the lost country
at the mouth of dreams
its jujube eruptions
its persistence bronze
with eternity
in a fragmentary illumination

with this absence
now at its hyperbolic threshold
engaging the shadow on a ground
that whitewashed stones and spergula
demarcate against its will
on which a presumed clearing
is barely hemmed in
nearly the place to imagine oneself
without home without memory
without so much as the evocation of a possible return
in a different time
one's night hoisted like a catafalque
on bared shoulders
to finally accede
to the recitation alternating
stars and suns freezing
into this very writing
where this cosmicity is silenced

simplement réalité intermédiaire
pour une mitoyenneté au paysage
de ses généalogies déjà mortes
et pour demeurer au loin
reliquat de nuit épars
dans des lieux d'errance qui se nient

simply intermediary reality
for a partitioning in the landscape
of its already dead genealogies
and to stay in the distance
remainder of scattered night
in self-denied regions of wandering

Le propre du ciel
est de reprendre
l'ample champ de l'éveil
quelque part
magie du bleu surnageant
en théorèmes denses

il faudrait un voisinage
comme la Mer des Crises
pour soupçonner dans des roses de sable
tant d'ailleurs concréfiés
depuis des neurones d'air

chaque lieu est rendu
plus essentiel
avec son jeu d'ombre
à la surface

avec des mots qui ne sont plus
que glanures de songe
que reflets dramatisés où le soleil s'incarne
invariablement mort songée
parvenu à rééditer son descriptif d'astre

des mots avec ce qui reste
dans la langue
de péninsules arbitraires

4

The sky's defining feature
is to recapture
the ample field of waking
somewhere
magic of the blue lingering
in dense theorems

only in a locality
like the Sea of Crises
could one sense in gypsum flowers
so many concrefied elsewheres
from airy neurons

each place is made
more essential
with its play of shadows
on the surface

with words now little more
than dream gleanings
than dramatized reflections where the sun incarnates itself
invariably dreamt death
having successfully reedited its starry description

words with whatever
arbitrary peninsulas
the language still possesses

de fable recommencée
avec des émergences
cumulus en découpe
au profil inséparable
d'une antériorité vaine

c'est le même voyage
qui ne veut pas finir
fondé en un mécanisme
de territoires épisodiques
où recule en proportion
l'oubli des racines
et qui engage sous des matins brefs
l'excédent de géographie
pour demeurer au milieu immobile
à rendre une parcellisation en steppes mortes
où le ciel s'agglutine
sans être le centre de tous les périples

où l'équivocité du jour est saisie tremblée
dans une récession marine
où pour associer sa quête
et le sentiment de son débris répétitif
il y a des sols en marge
avec la révélation continue
du même pays réfractaire
qui voudrait qu'un voisinage d'éternité
se dégage d'estrémadures lointaines
capturées dans le vide de la rétine

of fable begun again
with emergences
cut-out cumulus
with a profile inseparable
from a vain precedence

it is the same journey
which refuses to end
founded in a mechanism
of episodic territories
where the forgetting of roots
withdraws proportionally
engaging the surplus geography
under brief mornings
so as to stay in the middle immobile
to render a parcellation in dead steppes
where the sky agglutinates
without being the center of all voyages

where the day's equivocality is grasped trembled
in a marine recession
where to associate its quest
and the feeling of its repetitive debris
there are soils on the fringe
with the continuous revelation
of the same unyielding country
which would have an eternal locality
disengage from distant estremaduras
captured in the retina's emptiness

hauteurs restées dominées
d'encre de souvenance
et auxquelles il faut que je prodigue
espace gravité matière phénoménale
l'ordonnance de l'horizon et le parcours
suranné des idiomes que je porte

heights still dominated
by ink of recollection
which I must lavish with
space gravity phenomenal matter
the organization of the horizon and the outdated
course of the idioms I bear

Prescience d'écume
nouvelle fugue dans la matière
itinéraire prolongé jusqu'à l'exil

il suffit d'une rumeur océane
pour que l'instant procède
du large indispensable
à toute rêverie dispersée

compensation
en golfes de Sicile
au regard de milliers de syllabes erratiques
de haltes promises
et c'est tout un ciel à rebours
avec la remontée de régions mortes en reliefs
comme narration d'un possible dosage du réel

ici même il y avait une île
où se profilait jadis un passant sans mémoire
toujours pâle
dont la gestuelle était
parodie renouvelée de la fin des temps
appropriation d'une refonte des étoiles
il y avait une étendue rouillée
jusqu'à un espace pressenti
comme substance onirique une matière d'âme
dont les eaux reprenaient mille soleils révolus
autant que vomis par l'oxyrhinque noir de mes récits

Foresight of sea spray
new flight into matter
itinerary extended to the point of exile

one ocean murmur is enough
for the instant to proceed
from the open sea essential
to all scattered daydreams

compensation
in gulfs of Sicily
under the gaze of thousands of erratic syllables
of promised pauses
and it's a whole sky backwards
with the ascent from dead regions in relief
as narration of a possible dose of the real

on this very spot was an island
where long ago an oblivious passerby emerged
always pale
whose body language was
renewed parody of the end of time
appropriation of a recasting of stars
there was a rust-colored expanse
leading to a space foreseen
as dream substance a soul-like matter
whose waters recovered a thousand bygone suns
as many as spit up the black oxyrhynch of my tales

aujourd'hui elles sont assimilation graduelle
à une identité éphémère
sa réplique au-dedans conjecturée par ce qui se pose
en fin dernière dans une strophe
de rédemption à l'aube
à partir d'un contact simulé de la pierre

fascination morne
antinomie liée à un principe d'exclusion
où se confondent
indistinctement récit désir doute
alternance du vécu et du recommencé
une éternité d'images récurrentes
dont chaque reprise est investiture du corps
par sa variante assombrie

le corps frappé de ce mirage répétitif
qui est pour une liaison plus claire à la mort
le corps inhabité toutes ses origines reculées
vers sa nuit inaugurale
avec des nuages d'intercession pour un devenir
selon des écritures inconnues

today they are gradual assimilation
to an ephemeral identity
its replica conjectured within by that which is put down
as final end in a stanza
of redemption at dawn
from a simulated contact with stone

dismal fascination
antinomy bound to an exclusionary principle
in which tale desire doubt
commingle indistinctly
alternating the experienced and begun again
an eternity of recurrent images
whose every repetition is nomination of the body
by its darkened variation

the body struck by this repetitive mirage
which is for a clearer corelation with death
the body uninhabited its origins' sum withdrawn
toward its inaugural night
with clouds of intercession for an evolution
according to unknown writings

6

L'alphabet jadis bu est devenu lieu qui se retrace
de sa concordance avec la station de la pierre
de la confidence du voyageur et aussi du voyage
comme compromis avec le désert des haltes
par le simulacre
de Lixus
quand la circularité de l'instance
l'assimile au mot mort
tenu pour monère au présent

jamais réciprocité n'a agi sur le mot mort
avec une telle compensation du débris
une telle condensation dans le recul jusqu'à
une matière hors d'atteinte
n'a pu rappeler à l'adhérence
des falaises argumentant tour à tour le basalte
ou un ciel de cruauté qui surmonte
les collines régulées depuis un âge profond
mangeuses de mes paupières dévoreuses de mes siestes
c'est partant de l'intérieur que le site d'emblée s'adapte
cumul hypnagogique de soleil
à essaimer seulement en apparence sur des vagues

quelle écume ne serait alors hypothèse de son drame
ou pour moi vaste et indicible négation
du sel et du sable
sur des préalables confus de squelette

6

The alphabet once absorbed has become a self-depicting place
from its concordance with the position of stone
from the secret of the traveler and the travel
as compromise with the halt-filled desert
by the simulacra
of Lixus
when the circularity of entreaties
assimilates it to the dead word
the assumed moneron in the present

never has reciprocity acted on the dead word
with such compensation for debris
such condensation in the withdrawl back to
an unreachable matter
unable to call to adherence
successive cliffs arguing basalt
or a cruel sky surmounting
hills regulated deep ages ago
that have fed on my eyelids devoured my siestas
setting out from the interior the site instantly adapts
hypnagogic accumulation of sun
to swarming only apparently on waves

what sea spray would fail to be the hypothesis of its drama
or for me vast and unspeakable negation
of salt and sand
on confused skeletal preliminaries

quelle identité si ce n'est
imaginée
pèlerinage réminiscence le même rivage prégnant
dans la même perspective fuyante
quelle réintégration de soi
ici même que ne résumerait un arbre bruissant de ses cigales

quel éveil aux oléandres
si la mémoire est toujours en partance
de manière à ne pouvoir
se dire qu'énonciation résiduelle
le crâne prolongé d'un manège ivre d'oiseaux
comme du propos obscur de l'instant impossible à vivre
autrement qu'interférence dans le brassage du jour
situant ailleurs le palmier surérogatoire
et plus loin encore la genèse du réel

what identity if not
imagined
pilgrimage reminiscence the same pregnant shore
in the same receding perspective
what reintegration of the self
left unsummarized on this very spot by a tree buzzing with its cicadas

what awakening to oleanders
if memory is forever departing
so as to be able
to utter only residual enunciations
the elongated skull of a bird-drunk carousel
as with the obscure word of a moment unlivable
except as interference in the brewing of the light
situating elsewhere the supererogatory palm tree
and further still the genesis of the real

Celui qui arrive au bord de ses pays répandus
lit l'appartenance dans ce qui change à perte de vue
avec la prédominance du matin le ciel associe
effraction du jujubier évasion durée analogies
mais ce n'est pas le ciel qui installe la mise en ordre
c'est son image qui surplombe une mémoire tue

perception à la surface qui est
appropriation de généalogies éperdues
en profondeur éclatement du temps
dans ma langue extériorité des mots comme autant
d'ères migrantes qui s'originent d'elles-mêmes s'excluent

je veux pouvoir interroger sur un songe
cette cessation brusque des nuages au-dessus
des deltas de l'Amante où s'égarent mes cris
dire à la fois le lieu qui s'agence mal au vécu
et le vécu rendu à l'exercice de l'immensité
poussé à son seuil erratique
au nulle part chaque jour plus accentué devenu
du ressort d'oiseaux traversant
les crépuscules de mes rites abolis

7

He who arrives at the edge of his widespread lands
reads belonging in changes that stretch as far as the eye can see
the sky associates morning's dominance with
jujube break in escape duration analogies
but it is not the sky that establishes order
its image overhanging a silenced memory does

surface perception which is
appropriation of distraught genealogies
in depth time's rupture
in my language exteriority of words like so many
migrant eras originating from and excluding themselves

I want to ask about a dream
this sudden cessation of clouds overhead
the Lover's deltas where my cries stray
to express both the place in dissonance with experience
and experience given over to the exercise of immensity
pushed to its erratic threshold
to the nowhere each day more emphatic now
the responsibility of birds crossing
the twilights of my abolished rituals

une simulation du bleu qui accapare l'ailleurs
en moi où qu'il se replie
cette coalescence de nuit
autour d'un lexique de vieilles parentés
tout un patrimoine du sommeil et de l'éveil
incorporé à mon ombre revenue
se découvrant des contours d'arbres incandescent

a simulation of blue monopolizing the elsewhere
in me wherever it folds back
this coalescence of night
around a lexicon of old kinships
an entire patrimony of sleep and waking
incorporated into my shadow come back
realizing its incandescent tree outlines

La mesure de l'éveil
c'est l'échéance du matin
qui esquisse au passage
une ménopause de lunes
s'éloigne
et s'éloigne en même temps la citadelle
le paysage où se dire
ouvertement de nulle part
bien qu'avancé dans le possible
approximation de parhélie à apparence
jusqu'à l'anémone hurlée de mes lampes

c'est une image qui se recentre
dans l'écrit remis à l'épreuve de ses marges
ensuite qui s'efface
progressivement convaincue d'encriers à mort
et mot à boire définitif
pour la reprise dans la distance
de l'idiome qui lui tient lieu de réceptacle
et qui est déjà territorialité risquée
aux dépens de la mémoire

c'est de là que s'instaure
cette exaspération du désertique
à la façon d'une expansion sèche
circonscrivant le tenant du visage
les cheveux depuis la plante
l'altitude des membres
qu'il en est comme d'un écart de réel

The measure of awakening
is the term of morning
which in passing sketches
a lunar menopause
moves away
and the citadel moves away at the same time
the landscape where one can openly
admit to being from nowhere
though deep into the possible
an approximation of appearance parhelion
as far as the anemone howled by my lamps

it is an image that recenters itself
in the text challenged again by its margins
then disappearing
progressively convinced of fatal inkwells
and definitive word to drink
for the distant reprise
of the idiom serving as its receptacle
and which is already a territoriality risked
at the expense of memory

that is where
this exasperation of the desert space is established
like a dry expansion
circumscribing the face's disciple
the hair from the plant
the altitude of the limbs
such that it resembles a shift in the real

où immoler sa raison
pour consolider les impulsions de l'errance
d'un espace de part en part traversé de son doute
pour que mon nom soit de transhumance
d'inadéquation partant de maternités
cruelles dans l'amarante
d'inaliénable mer couvant
sous la distribution des tertres

pour qu'il ne reste que des morceaux de ciel
en délirium fragmenté sur la table
régression manifeste
d'une carte vieillie dans le parcours théologique
et de plus en plus rétrécie la texture
abolie de pays à ne risquer au dehors ni infini
ni cœur en nébuleuse béante
ascèse à oublier la nuit et son hypothèse
dans le parenchyme développant l'avancée
de mille saisons néantes

in which to immolate one's reason
so as to consolidate the impulses of wandering
from a space crossed through by one's doubt
that my name may be of transhumance
of inadequacy setting out from cruel
maternities in the amaranth
of inalienable sea simmering
under the distribution of burial mounds

so that only pieces of sky remain
fragmented in delirium on the table
manifest regression
of a map become obsolete on the theological path
and more and more constricted the abolished
texture of a country to risk neither without nor infinity
nor heart as gaping nebula
asceticism to forget the night and its hypothesis
in the developing parenchyma the advance
of one thousand naught seasons

9

Un désert approximatif mais activé
dans sa primauté sur toute autre étendue
en attendant que mon silence
puisse l'introduire

vastitude pour s'épargner malentendus autour
des sépultures
des incarnations de villes
de plus en plus méconnaissables
dès qu'on en interprète l'inflation des ruines

autour des figurations de la pierre finissant d'absorber tout le site
        telluries hâves
ébauchées d'un système de mer nomade
et parcellaires des mêmes mots des mêmes fragments
au fur et à mesure du corps que j'habite

voisinage somnambulique dont se tire l'essentiel
de cette signification d'hégémonie évaluée à son ascendant
sur la dérive de la pupille
dans une proximité telle
que les plaines mêmes de midi ne m'atteignent plus

et sans que je sache qui de cette instance
ou de mon ventricule
fond ensemble l'être et le paraître
brouille dans les errances de l'encre
les âges suspendus au-dessus d'architectures
en butte aux griefs du vent et la solitude l'écrit

9

A desert approximate yet activated
in its primacy over any other expanse
until such time as my silence
may announce it

the immensity to spare itself misunderstandings about
sepulchers
incarnations of cities
increasingly unrecognizable
as soon as their inflated ruins are interpreted

around figurations of stone absorbing the entire site
        haggard telluriums
sketched out by a nomadic oceanic system
and splintered into the same words the same fragments
little by little into the body I inhabit

somnambulistic vicinity whose essence is extracted
from this hegemonic meaning evaluated at its ascendance
on the pupillary drift
in a proximity such
that the very plains of noon no longer reach me

and without my knowing who of this body
or of my ventricle
fuses being and semblance
blurs in inky meanders
the ages suspended over architectural structures
exposed to the grievances of the wind and solitude writing

ou si la raison entièrement caduque
à la recension de cet espace où le cœur est libre
de polariser le retour des nuées
s'est nantie de nouvelles amnésies
s'est aggravée d'étoiles disparues
toutes des galaxies qu'elle fige
en majoliques
pour la célébration du soupir et l'âpreté de la supplique

c'est le prolongement du même territoire à vif
au paroxysme des ratures
songerie ponctuée de mille ailleurs
comme alternative à une nuit
enclavée dans les vertèbres
avec le sentiment de cette mesure expectante
liée à la propagation de pays apocryphes
confondue avec l'irruption du lentisque
l'oubli des origines
et comme ordre de réfutation dans une souveraineté de l'aride

itinéraire échappé à des régions autrement
plus amovibles
majeur de ses intermittences réfractaire de ses racines
arrière-pays dans la mouvance du prétérit
pour peu que mon dire s'articule
par le biais du méandre générique
dans une persistance ténue de voûtes fossilisées
où le ciel définitivement clos
s'est scellé de gageures en terre cuite
dominé d'une parenté avec l'autre ciel poursuivant
au-dessus des palmiers une bleuité coercitive

or if reason wholly obsolete
at the recension of this space where the heart is free
to polarize the clouds' return
has armed itself with new amnesias
aggravated by vanished stars
all of them galaxies that it fixes
in maiolica
to celebrate the sigh and the bitterness of the petition

it is the extension of the same raw territory
to the climax of deletions
reverie punctuated by a thousand elsewheres
as alternative to a single night
enclosed in the vertebrae
with the feeling of this expectant measure
bound to the propagation of apocryphal lands
commingled with the eruption of the lentiscus
the forgetting of origins
and as refutation order in a sovereignty of the arid

itinerary fled from otherwise more
detachable regions
important for its intermittences refractory for its roots
back country in the mobility of the preterit
if only my claim were articulated
through the angle of generic meandering
in a sustained persistence of fossilized archways
in which the permanently closed sky
was sealed with terra cotta wagers
dominated by a relationship with the other sky pursuing
above the palm trees a coercive blueness

et qui est en marge pour n'être ni au dedans ni au dehors
dégagé d'un reliquat d'aube mais subordonné
à des ruptures de traversée
alors que toute autre réalité s'est changée
en dunes répétitives
qu'elle oscille entre les limites de l'écriture
et l'horizon profondément établi de rivages antithétiques
assignant la vue à des tombes
submergées de nuit paradoxale

comme s'inscrivant
en une durée séparée
qui nous vaut d'être oppressés
de périmètres aux buissons occultés
d'autant plus éponymes qu'ils se définissent mal
sous la réticence des monticules

notre contemplation ira sans cesse du côté de ces villes
subjuguées du ralenti des vagues
résignées aux stridulations que s'attache encore
le roncier depuis le parcours d'origine
aux prises avec des agrégats
très vite assimilés
à de nouvelles constellations du remords
pour la connaissance et le patrimoine
où puisse s'exercer quelque injonction d'étoiles à venir

durée seule qui pourrait avoir la propriété d'insinuer
dans les monceaux discordants de nos squelettes
de vagues frémissements
comme des impulsions fugitives
comme si nous étions
accessoirement plongés dans des rêves

which exists on the fringe so as to be neither within nor without
disengaged from an auroral remainder but subordinate
to disruptions of crossing
while every other reality has turned
into repetitive dunes
that it oscillates between the limits of writing
and the deeply established horizon of antithetical shorelines
attributing sight to graves
submerged in paradoxical night

as if inscribing itself
in a separate duration
for which we are oppressed
by perimeters with eclipsed shrubs
all the more eponymous in their lack of definition
beneath the reticence of hillocks

our contemplation will ever drift toward those cities
subjugated by the waves' slow motion
resigned to the chirring still clinging
to brambles from the initial path
at odds with aggregates
immediately assimilated
to new constellations of remorse
for the knowledge and patrimony
in which some injunction of coming stars may be exercised

duration alone that might bear the quality of insinuating
into the discordant mounds of our skeletons
vague tremblings
like fleeting impulses
as if we were
incidentally thrust into dreams

des rêves déplaçant des tentes par milliers
des territoires par milliers et que nos sédiments miraculés
tout d'un coup pouvaient
se mettre à dispenser l'éveil
survolés de sa dimension vibratile
comme si elle était diffusée depuis une remémoration profonde
réfractée du bain stellaire à l'origine de nébuleuses errantes
et qui n'a d'ancrage nulle part
n'est pas complexité organique faisant un corps stationnaire des
    saisons antérieures
ou réclusion qui préoccupe le devenir au terme de chaque voyage
ou qui implique à la faveur de l'antimoine
le pathétique d'un pur visage de légende
mais pour venir à nous malgré les suspensions de méridiens
comme haut lieu de syzygies comme prérogative
du genévrier sur la colline
comme perception de ces géographies
tout à la fois paramnésie que vicissitude d'ombre
repliée dans une instance éloignée

ultime compensation de la pierre attentive
dans son atonie
à quelque divinité éparse
et avec elle l'espace voué aux paradoxes du refus
sans les déambulations de naguère
sans toutes ces méditations
à partir de l'absence de citadelles et le mental
coupé de son eau première

*C'est la vanité des transitions pour celui dont l'identité est presque
excédentaire de tant de lieux de pure latence ;
il y a comme une irréalité dans cette multiplication des repères, com-
me un paysage de plus en plus désordonné par rapport à l'éveil, un*

dreams displacing tents by the thousands
territories by the thousands and that our miracular sediments
could suddenly
begin to radiate waking
overflown by its vibratile dimension
as if it were diffused from some deep recollection
refracted from the stellar bath at the source of wandering nebulæ
with nowhere to anchor
is not organic complexity forging a stationary body from
     anterior seasons
or reclusion preoccupying evolution at the end of each journey
or which through the use of antimony implies
the pathos of a pure legendary face
but in order to reach us in spite of meridian suspensions
as center of syzygies as prerogative
of the hill-borne juniper
as perception of these geographies
simultaneously paramnesia and shadowy vagaries
withdrawn into distant entreaties

ultimate compensation of stone attentive
in its atony
to some scattered divinity
and with it space devoted to the paradoxes of refusal
without the deambulations of former times
without all of these meditations
from the absence of citadels and the mindset
cut off from its original water

It is the vanity of transitions for him whose identity is nearly ex-
ceeded by so many purely latent places;
there is something like an irreality in this multiplication of reference
points, like a landscape increasingly chaotic in relation to waking, a

ciel comme atteint d'excentricité dans ses molécules disparates, il y a comme un horizon fragmenté,

il n'y a même plus de voyageur pour se postuler à travers des régions autrement douées de vertus de scissiparité, fécondées à l'infini, que le jour et la nuit en sont méconnaissables ; il s'instaure comme un désir de proclamer l'avènement des dissemblances, de réinventer pour la consolidation des signes comme une heure d'apocalypse imminente et un attachement à ressusciter des nostalgies transfigurées pour une nouvelle chaîne des appartenances, avec l'introduction de la leçon d'ectoplasme pour l'ombre métallique qu'il étalera par dessus la lisibilité du désespoir et pour la preuve qui, sur l'appel impérieux du désert, fonde les brûlures.

Il n'y a de pèlerinage que rétrospectif d'une démarche où se sont associées des géographies cognitives et l'instance de l'ombre qui servira d'emblée à les démentir ;

comme un lieu perceptible dans ses variations, un lieu qui est mot crépusculaire dessaisi de ses racines, aux voyages rendus hybrides et d'autant plus intraitable qu'il dissipe progressivement tout le spectre de la réalité qui en consolide le patrimoine – œil putride du soleil fixé définitivement sur des mers usurpées, témoin de la fossilisation de toutes ces étendues placentaires dont l'ingérence a trempé l'âme de ma langue dans le rire et le blasphème.

Il n'y a que des haltes, des perspectives isolées dans la récurrence d'une même approximation du dehors, il n'y a qu'un espace égal où la géométrie du jour déplace la même fascination de l'aride dans une mémoire des choses qui n'est plus.

Tout est songerie, image, métamorphose, convulsion de nuages, processus de déréliction à ne pouvoir offrir que son mutisme en pâture aux terrains vagues ;

toute cette réitération de moments à la limite du vécu, de haltes comparatives, de rêves contradictoires,

tout est dérivation d'un même et unique propos placé comme s'il était chaque matin le fait d'une nouvelle articulation des fièvres et

*sky seemingly suffering from eccentricity in its disparate molecules,
there is something like a fragmented horizon,*

*there are no more travelers that we might postulate ourselves through
regions otherwise endowed with schizogenic virtues, infinitely fertile,
that day and night are unrecognizable; it is established like a desire
to declare the advent of dissimilarities, to reinvent for the consolida-
tion of signs something like an hour of imminent apocalypse and
an affection for reviving transfigured nostalgias for a new chain
of affiliations, with the introduction of the lesson in ectoplasm for
the metallic shadow it will spread over the legibility of despair, and
for the evidence which, on the imperious call of the desert, initiates
burns.*

*There are only pilgrimages in retrospect of a process combining cog-
nitive geographies and the entreaties of shadow which will immedi-
ately serve to refute them;*

*something like a place perceptible in its variations, a place that is
twilight word divorced from its roots, with journeys made hybrid
and all the more uncompromising that it gradually dispels the entire
spectrum of reality which consolidates its patrimony – putrid eye
of the sun riveted on usurped seas, witness to the fossilization of all
these placental expanses whose interference has steeped the soul of
my language in laughter and blasphemy.*

*There are only halts, perspectives isolated in the recurrence of a sin-
gle approximation of the outside, there is only one equivalent space
where the geometry of day displaces the same fascination with the
arid in a memory of things which no longer exists.*

*All is reverie, image, metamorphosis, convulsion of clouds, pro-
cess of dereliction with only its silence to offer as pasture to waste
lands;*

*all this reiteration of moments at the limit of experience, compara-
tive halts, contradictory dreams,*

*all is derivation of a single, unique remark placed as if each morn-
ing it were the fact of a new articulation of fevers and no longer the*

non plus le lieu privilégié où puissent s'évacuer la lune, les étoiles, s'ouvrir d'autres soleils comme de hautes et immenses pivoines ;

tout est accaparé de contrées diffuses, sans plus de place pour les généalogies perdues, les latitudes fondamentales, ni le pays dans sa projection d'arbre ennuagé en mesure d'entretenir la confidence jusqu'à sa dérive loin très loin jusque dans la sieste du bidonville.

Tout est négation, prise en charge d'une traversée devenue elle-même hypothétique, hasard contingent, expulsion mémorielle, sacrement d'amnésie, par un système d'épandage de fleurs naïves, de fleurs en cinabre et indigo peinturlurant le bois de hautes et antiques horloges comme autant de machines à ponction de délirium, et qui maintiennent jusqu'à l'aube l'activité d'un récit où se profilent incidemment oliviers sauvages et sous-bois constellés de cistes ;

tout est négation, simulacre, désert sous-jacent, exégèse du souvenir n'ayant d'autre finalité que le souvenir en soi, qui englobe l'Iram-aux-colonnes et les sanctuaires abritant des corps imputrescibles, celui exhibé pour la compréhension des êtres et des choses, celui culminant dès l'irruption de montagnes psycho-cosmiques en vue de la déréalité des parcours, des saisons, et pour agir de l'infiniment petit à l'infiniment grand en effaçant toute trace de devenir ;

tout est circonscrit à l'étroitesse du soupir, à un rituel méthodique qui reprend uniformément fantasmes, classifications folkloriques, métaphores comme sacralisation du débris, poupées attifées de grelots, la durée embaumée, subliminale, aux vertus talismaniques, en un même et unique cycle des larmes et de l'abandon ;

tout est hantise de mille séances consacrées à ces ultimes chroniques relatant des périples catalogués comme répertoire d'illusion et d'agonie, et dont l'écoute est infinie, qui est comme une rumeur des siècles venant s'échouer près de ma mémoire en une succession de topographies qui voyagent, irradiantes de soleils perdus, d'étoiles chancelantes, avec un ciel paraissant être le prolongement d'un songe qui ne veut pas finir et étalé sur des étendues insoutenables puis porté toujours plus loin par des dorsales en dérive ;

privileged place through which the moon and stars may be evacuated, other suns may open like towering peonies;

all is monopolized by diffused lands, leaving no place for lost genealogies, fundamental latitudes, nor the country in its projection as a cloud-wrapped tree capable of fostering confidence as far as its distant very distant drift as far as the slum's siesta.

All is negation, charge taking of a crossing itself now hypothetical, contingent chance, memory expulsion, amnesic sacrament, through a system of manuring naïve flowers, flowers cinnabar and indigo splashing the wood of tall, ancient clocks like so many delirium-draining machines that pursue until dawn the activity of a story in which wild olive trees and cyst-constellated underbrush are serendipitously shaped;

all is negation, simulacrum, underlying desert, exegesis of memory with no other finality than memory itself, which encompasses Iram of the Pillars and the sanctuaries housing imputrescible bodies, the one exhibited for the understanding of beings and things, the one peaking the very moment psycho-cosmic mountains erupt in preparation for the dereality of paths, of seasons, and to act from the infinitely small to the infinitely large while erasing all traces of evolution;

all is confined to the narrowness of a sigh, to a methodic ritual that uniformly resumes fantasies, folk typologies, metaphors as sacralization of debris, dolls adorned with tiny bells, embalmed, subliminal duration with talismanic virtues, in a single, unique cycle of tears and abandon;

all is obsession with a thousand meetings devoted to these final chronicles relating voyages cataloged as a repertoire of illusion and agony, whose listening is infinite, which is like a distant sound of centuries running aground near my memory in a succession of traveling topographies, radiant with lost suns, faltering stars, with a sky seeming the extension of a dream that refuses to end, spread out over unsustainable expanses then carried ever further away by drifting dorsal fins;

c'est tout le présent qui se mettrait à chavirer pour perdre instantané-
ment de sa consistance, de sa rassurante proximité ; on est soi-même
en situation de complète distorsion par rapport à son propre acquis
existentiel ; il n'y a ni début ni fin ni parcours comme si l'origine de
toute chose s'enveloppait d'une espèce de nuit mercurielle exsudée de
confins maritimes

durée à tout moment renouvelée
de son réseau de séquences en rupture
pléthore de dunes à la périphérie du silence
qui ne peut s'inscrire
que frontalière de régions saisies en images identiques
dans un dire impossible
qui tire ses ressources
de sa propre matière de déplacement
du même lieu toujours extrême
avoisinant celui des racines

qui est ce nulle part dont le désert
à mes côtés est l'incidence éclatée
comme un moi allégorique
qui n'en finit pas d'être multiple

and the entire present would begin to keel over, instantly losing some
of its consistency, its reassuring proximity; we ourselves are in a
situation of complete distortion with respect to our own existential
knowledge; there is no beginning no end no path as if the origin of
each thing were shrouded in a sort of mercurial night exuded by
coastal borders

duration constantly renewed
by its network of ruptured sequences
plethora of dunes on the periphery of silence
which can only be inscribed
as frontier zone of regions caught in identical images
in an impossible claim
which draws its resources
from its own displacement matter
from the same, always extreme place
bordering that of roots

which is this nowhere whose desert
at my side is the shattered incidence
like an allegorical I
that never stops being multiple

Divan de la mer obscure

DARK SEA DIVAN

Unpublished · EXCERPTS

❖

*Translated by Guy Bennett, Addie Leak
and Teresa Villa-Ignacio*

FUGUE EN DISPERSION MAJEURE

Voici l'ombre promenée telle qu'auprès de ses semblables
elle devrait normalement figurer à longueur de temps :
paisible et homogène, la température au repos sur la grève.
Le fait est que nous ne soyons jamais parvenus
en dépit des régimes d'intimité immédiate
et des règles de mitoyenneté consensuelle,
à l'engagement formel qu'elle devait se borner
à la même géométrie rigoureuse
à cette même surface ruisselée qui avance maintenant
pas à pas dans le drame solaire.

Il y a bien longtemps, par un matin comme il y en a tant
où le cœur sans raison apparente s'emplit de larmes,
je l'ai observée cependant que les contours singulièrement tremblés,
elle avait hasardé une incursion hésitante près de ce champ maritime
souvent de délimitation incertaine et qui affranchit, dit-on,
des liens avec le rivage, engage le péril des métamorphoses.

Nous avions toujours jusque-là été favorisés de cette symétrie
constante qui guide tout naturellement en direction des terrains
vagues ; elle nous permettait d'évoluer au gré du vent, de l'impensé,
à ciel ouvert, tous deux pénétrés du climat des pourpiers, humectés
du sel des embruns ; d'être à travers nos chuchotements, nos vécus
réciproques, chaque fois submergés d'une communion prolongée
dans les ténèbres.

FUGUE IN DISPERSION MAJOR

Here is the shadow paraded such as next to its own
it should normally appear over time:
calm, uniform, its temperature at rest on the strand.
The fact is that despite systems
of closest intimacy and rules
of consensual adjacency, we never achieved
the formal commitment that it limit itself
to the same rigorous geometry
to that same streamed surface now advancing
step by step into the solar drama.

A very long time ago, on a morning like so many others
when the heart for no apparent reason fills with tears,
I observed it and its oddly trembled outlines,
it had risked a hesitant incursion near this coastal field
often of uncertain delimitation and that frees, it is said,
from bonds to the shore, engages the danger of metamorphoses.

Until then we had always been favored by this unchanging
symmetry which leads quite naturally to wastelands; it would
allow us to move with the wind, with the unthought, in the open
air, both of us permeated with the climate of purslane, moistened
with the salt of sea spray; to be through our whisperings, our recip-
rocal experiences, submerged each time in a prolonged communion
with the shadows.

Elle avait ce jour-là revêtu toute la gamme des nuances qui devaient la conforter dans son statut de compagne errante – son espace invariant, à chaque empan recommencé, établi en site magnifié du possible où s'écoute la houle et se manifeste, en puissance, à corps-perdu, la transition vers les rives d'une hyperbole.

C'est alors qu'elle fut soudain dispersée, comme sujette à des évasions subies ; et j'étais cet homme pâle qui se vidait de sa substance alors que ses linéaments à mes côtés, au fur et à mesure dévidés, cherchaient leur synthèse avec une nappe maculée de limon, parsemée de méduses opalines ; je ne sais déjà plus combien de temps a pu durer cette étrange défection, ce voyage de toutes les absences car près de moi tout n'était qu'excentricité, dérive et machination d'eau mêlée à une lumière noire.

Depuis lors
nos flâneries connaissent maintes ruptures, quantité de turbulences comme si elles s'exerçaient toutes et séparément sous des latitudes paradoxales. À l'aller comme au retour sont revues à l'examen de l'océan, à la preuve par ces amples flux de mémoire qui font la rumeur de sept mers cumulées respirant ensemble

        dans la trame d'un seul verset

                en offrande au crépuscule.

That day it had assumed the full range of subtleties destined to
confirm it in its status as nomadic companion – its unvarying
space, begun again with each span, established as a magnified site
of the possible where the sea swell is heard and, surging, with all its
might, the transition toward the banks of a hyperbole seen.

That is when it was suddenly dispersed, as subject to sustained
escapes; and I was that pale man emptying himself of his substance
while by my side, its features gradually uncoiled, sought their
synthesis with a spattered layer of silt, strewn with opaline jellyfish;
and I have already forgotten how long this strange abandonment
may have lasted, this journey of every absence for near me all was
but eccentricity, drift, and watery conspiracy mixed with black
light.

Since then
our amblings have known many interruptions, much turbulence as
if collectively and separately they were being carried out in paradoxi-
cal parts of the world. Coming and going are reviewed on the ocean's
examination, on the evidence by these ample fluxes of memory that
spread the rumor of seven accumulated seas breathing together
            in the framework of a single verse
                        as an offering to twilight.

G B

EN MARGE

Avant que la silhouette ne s'imprègne
de ce qui va lui donner contour et épaisseur
la saturer d'écriture de temps statique,
la consolider à l'échelle de son tombeau,
à cet instant on a envie que les jours passés
ou ce qui reste encore des jours passés,
– après la vague perception de leur fuite
entre tumulte océanique et ombres dilatées,
jusqu'où l'horizon se faisait déchirure –
on a envie de voir toute cette part d'absence
reconduite aux confins du cœur ennuagé
et mise en phase avec des décans ésotériques.

Ensuite, une fois tout accompli que le ciel
en reprise aérienne se reconfigure
dans son incarnat de naguère retrouvé,
puis qu'il se mette au jour et à l'heure
où il fut permis, depuis un vol d'étourneaux
en longue suspension dans la brise,
de sentir se dissiper les lois invisibles
qui participent de l'immédiateté de soi –
ce jour où il a fallu rentrer en hâte avec
le bourgeonnement précipité d'un distique
éperdu (maintenant à jamais évanoui)
poignant d'origine et qui anticipait l'illimité.

ON THE MARGIN

Before the silhouette soaks up
what will give it contour and thickness
saturate it with writing of static time,
fortify it on the scale of its tomb,
at this instant we want for past days
or what remains of past days,
– after the vague perception of their flight
between oceanic tumult and dilated shadows,
to the place where the horizon ripped itself open –
we want to see that whole share of absence
led back to the confines of a clouded heart
and tuned to match esoteric decans.

Then, when everything is done may the sky
in an aerial reprise cloak itself again
in its newly remembered crimson,
and position itself at the day and time
when it was permitted, from a flight of starlings
suspended long on the breeze,
to sense the invisible laws making up the
immediacy of the self dissipate –
that day that required a hasty return with
the sudden budding of a frantic
distich (now forever vanished)
poignant in origin and anticipating the boundless.

On a envie de tout quitter ; de s'en remettre
à l'appoint de cartes pâlissantes, à l'ombre
portée d'un brin de chaume au coin des lèvres
et d'emboîter le pas à ses mots en repli ;
de renoncer après tant de prodiges à ces voix
aux harmoniques incorrompues, ces pastorales
atlasiques que des femmes en cheveux
mélangeaient aux senteurs des prés
et offraient en breuvage aromatisé
pour le poème de métempsycose à réciter
aux derniers jours de l'humanité. Et encore partir
à s'en rendre méconnaissable étranger
au milieu de pans d'existence qui vous suivent
dans la poussière des banlieues asphyxiées,
vous dépassent en buissons errants
et vont se perdre dans la pâle analogie du soleil.

Quitter toutes ces autres voies silencieuses
qui enseignèrent aux uns à marcher pieds nus
vêtus de laine grossière, et à d'autres
préparés au déclin imminent des étoiles,
à se détourner du monde à aller on ne sait où ;
et à d'autres pour qui sagesse et folie
ont été parts égales d'un même vouloir vivre,
retirés dans une sombre et affreuse caverne,
à mettre la dernière main à leurs divorces ;
et à d'autres encore en proie à des doutes secrets
à se prévaloir de la présomption d'un ange
là-haut parmi les lueurs déclinantes qui pourrait
à tout moment atteindre d'impossibilité ; et eux
pendant ce temps se dire submergés de sa toute présence
et rester à l'ombre des ramures mouvantes
captifs d'un songe qui ne veut pas finir.

We want to leave everything behind; to trust to the
precise number of fading cards, in the shadow
projected by a wisp of straw in the corner of the mouth
and to fall in step with its words in retreat;
to renounce after so many miracles these voices
with their uncorrupted harmonies, these Atlas
pastorals that bareheaded women
mixed with the scents of the prairies
and offered as aromatic drink
for the metempsychosic poem to be recited
in humanity's last days. And again begin
to make ourselves unrecognizable foreign
in the parts of existence that follow you
in the dust of asphyxiated suburbs,
pass by you in wandering bushes
and will be lost in the pale analogy of the sun.

To leave all these other quiet paths
that teach some to walk barefoot
dressed in crude wool, and others
prepared for the looming decline of the stars,
to turn away from the world and go who knows where;
and to others for whom wisdom and madness
have been equal shares of the same desire to live,
tucked away in a dark dreadful cavern,
to put the final touches on their divorces;
and to others still prey to secret doubts
to invoke the conjecture of an angel
up there among the dissipating gleams who could
at any moment reach impossibility; and those during
this time calling themselves submerged in its all-presence
and staying in the shadow of moving branches
captives of a daydream that doesn't want to end.

Renouer en chemin avec ces mots tremblés
tels qu'hérités des perambulations solitaires,
respirant cette bienheureuse inconscience qui a
le propre de revêtir comme d'un voile de protection,
qui met la commissure en place pour l'inflexion
inhérente à l'énoncé du parti-pris d'errance ;
qui promène à la lisière de l'argile ténébreuse
à perte de vue dans l'armoise qui blanchit les steppes,
qui égare dans le vert tendre de la marjolaine sauvage
conduit à travers les plaines battues par les vents
aux premiers escarpements de rocaille calcaire,
puis aux maisons frustes en vieille tourbe grise
comme immobiles entre des milliers de tombes,
et d'où l'on revient submergé d'infini
non sans avoir eu à ravaler par moments
la montée brusque d'un pleur irraisonné.

Mais près des lieux disparus où peu s'en faut
que le paysage lui-même ne s'estompe à jamais,
où tout ce qui subsiste renvoie à la tension
des espaces qui se profilent derrière la tête,
relègue à l'orée introvertie du récit muet
aux contrées dévolues aux frôleurs de néant –
une fois là, tout autre itinéraire suspendu,
il faudra comme avant y bénir le lieu qui ranime
de l'autre côté, dans le livre de l'inaperçu,
le sentiment d'avoir encore été inséparable
du même interlocuteur invisible, le même
sur les chemins envahis de chardon vivace
le long de la broussaille amie des ruines,
qui sait donner un nom à l'émotion rêvée
qui se souvient de l'autre vie où œuvrent encore
des portions d'âme que nous croyions éteintes.

Reunite along the way with these words shivered
as though inherited from solitary perambulations,
breathing that blissful unconsciousness that clothes
itself in clean like a protective veil,
that puts lips in place for the bending
inherent in the uttered commitment to wandering;
that walks at the edge of the dark clay continuing
till out of sight in the wormwood whitening the steppes,
that gets lost in the wild marjoram's tender green
conducted across the wind-beaten plains
to the first escarpments of limestone rock,
then to the worn houses in old gray peat
as though stationary amid thousands of tombs,
and from which one returns submerged in the infinite
not without sometimes having had to
bite back the brusque rise of an irrational tear.

But near disappeared sites where it doesn't take much
for the landscape itself to dim forever,
where everything that remains harks back to the tension
of spaces profiled behind the head,
relegates to the mute narrative's introverted brink
to the lands destined to brushers against nothingness –
once there, all other itineraries on hold,
one must again bless that site that revives
from the other side, in the book of the unperceived,
the feeling of having again been inseparable
from the same invisible speaker, the same one
on the paths invaded by stubborn thistles
along the undergrowth friend of ruins,
who knows how to name a dreamed emotion
who remembers the other life where portions of the soul
we believed extinguished still strive.

AL

RETOUR

Si jamais revenaient nos vies anciennes
il n'est pas dit qu'elles seraient encore
sonores des mots disparus – des mots
qui avaient jadis peuplé le monde
qui venaient par hasard sur nos lèvres ;
ni qu'elles révèleraient depuis quand
nous ont été échus en émulsion de nuage
en chaos d'images aurorales,
le lot de ceux qui réverbéraient l'absence
et qui furent dépositaires d'apparences.

De ces mots portés à l'infini nous avons
marché attentifs à l'axe où nos pas d'hier
nous attendaient ; ensuite vers où nous avions
empoigné des rêves, laissé au vent la part
du vécu avec vue sur ortie et heures vides ;
des mêmes mots flottants, épars, nous avons
quêté l'aube comme instant empourpré
propice à l'adhérence des objets non pensés,
qui prend soin de cerner la subjectivité
qui exempte des chagrins de l'île déserte.

Si jamais revenaient nos vies anciennes
elles verraient à mi-chemin notre doublure
abstraite accrue d'un ici aveuglant,
présage de ciel blême et roses mourantes
subordonné à une syllabe de haute mer ;

RETURN

If ever our old lives came back
there's no knowing if they would still
ring with vanished words – words
that once peopled the world
and came by chance to our lips;
nor if they would reveal when
all those who echoed absence
and kept up appearances
expired before us in an emulsion of cloud
and a chaos of auroral images.

We walked away from these words angled to the infinite
mindful of the axis where yesterday's footsteps
awaited us; then towards the place we had
grabbed hold of dreams, left to the wind the share
of life overlooking stinging nettles and empty hours;
from the same floating, sparse words, we have
sought the dawn like a flushed instant
suitable for the cling of unthought-of objects,
which takes care to encircle the subjectivity
that exempts from desert island grief.

If ever our old lives came back
they would see halfway there our abstract
lining gathered from a blinding present,
omen of a pallid sky and dying roses
subordinate to a high-sea syllable;

elles nous verraient sur l'autre rive
en arrière-plan des remous brillants,
assignés aux errements de la verticalité,
dépouillés de nos biens, scrutant la barque
à emprunter pour le raccourci des songes.

they would see us on the other bank
as the backdrop of bright wake,
summoned to vertical wanderings,
stripped of our belongings, eyeing the boat
to borrow to shortcut daydreams.

AL

DÉRIVATION

Il reste quantité d'autres chemins
à parcourir, à ciel ouvert, sans lien,
revus à l'épreuve de l'immensité,
roses à l'aurore, écarlates le soir ;
pas forcément appelés à être mis
par tout un enchevêtrement d'idées
en équation avec un terrain vague,

ou à faire obligation de baptiser
les lieux disparus les nuits révolues
d'appellations d'amertume ; d'évoquer
une fois de plus les errances qui ont
mené au bord de la question absente
tandis qu'en route elles lancinaient
d'afflux de tendresse désespérée.

Que de villes traversées, d'horizons
dans la brume, de contrées dépassées
où l'on aurait voulu trouver refuge,
pour le motif qu'elles sont continues
jusqu'à l'océan et qu'il y est l'élément
ayant su préparer aux réciprocités
aériennes, aux latitudes incertaines.

DRIFT

Many more paths remain to be explored
under the open sky, disconnected,
revisited as proof against immensity,
pink at dawn, scarlet in the evening;
not necessarily called by a
whole entanglement of ideas
to equate to a vague terrain,

nor to require the baptism of
disappeared places bygone nights
with names of bitterness; to evoke
once more the rovings that have
led to the edge of the absent question
while along the way they tormented
with an influx of desperate tenderness.

So many crosscut cities, foggy
horizons, outmoded countries
where we wanted to find refuge
because they are continuous
unto the ocean because there it is the element
able to prepare for aerial
reciprocities, for latitudinal uncertanties.

On se dit avoir entrevu ces sortes
de fugues, d'étendues excommuniées,
comme des transferts extériorisés,
les seuls qui permettent tout à la fois
d'attendre et d'être déjà très loin,
qui laissent la voie libre aux scansions
natives en premier des profondeurs.

We tell ourselves we've encountered these kinds
of escapes, outcast stretches,
like externalized transferences
the only ones that make it possible to wait
while already being very far away,
that clear a path for native
scansions first of the depths.

TVI

POINT D'OCCULTATION

Voici la brèche par où s'est éloigné en s'évadant
hors de la conscience limite – l'être du voyage.
C'était le flâneur paradoxal même, quelqu'un
que le rapport à l'océan engageait à porter ses pas
machinalement, au fil des mots chuchotés,
à la bordure spectrale de sa propre présence ;
il se tenait loin de la survenue des ombres
disait qu'il avait là tout un dispositif de fugue
avec le bruit de la houle, un ciel buissonnier,
et des oiseaux en ronde au-dessus de la baie.

OCCULTATION POINT

Here is the breach through which it fled
escaping maximum consciousness – the being of the journey.
Having gradually become the paradoxical flâneur itself,
its relationship to the ocean moved it to make its way
mechanically, in the flow of whispered words,
to the spectral edge of its own presence;
it kept its distance from the oncoming shadows
said that it had an escape plan there
with the noise of the swell, a truant sky,
and a round of birds above the bay.

L'emplacement pour sa part a été localisé
au hasard du littoral, sur le même parcours
qui avait offert jadis au vécu comme au rêvé,
comme au gré des consonances bohémiennes,
d'avancer sans crainte dans la brume ensoleillée,
d'aller vers où la pierre a une teinte plus sombre
– cela bien avant la refonte du paysage –
là où tout se fond dans un ensemble rocheux
et où l'on peut à peine distinguer une béance
d'une autre béance qui donne sur le large.

The site itself was located randomly
on the coastline, on the same path
that had once allowed experience as it had dreams,
as if at the whim of bohemian consonances
to advance unafraid into the sunlit mist,
to move toward where the stone has a darker hue
– this well before the recasting of the landscape –
where all melds into a rocky ensemble
and where one may hardly distinguish one chasm
from another chasm that opens onto the sea.

On y accède à partir d'un lot de mégalithes
perdus dans le chaos granitique environnant,
et à la différence des rochers voisins on sent
que l'endroit participe d'un extérieur aveugle,
qu'il reproduit la matière même de l'absence ;
il délaie dans la part d'écume répandue
sur les récifs l'évidence du dedans et du dehors,
place d'emblée face à ce sentiment d'abandon
que tout homme après le retrait des vagues
continue de porter en silence.

You get there by way of several megaliths
lost in the surrounding granite chaos,
and unlike the neighboring rocks you feel
that the place belongs to a blind exterior,
that it reproduces the very matter of absence;
it dilutes the evidence of inside and outside
in the portion of foam spread over the reefs,
a place faced straightaway with that feeling of desertion
that every man after the receding of the waves
silently carries in himself.

Il arrive par moments que cet espace éparpillé,
tout en intermittence dans le scintillement aquatique,
paraisse comme hors d'atteinte. On s'imagine
qu'il a pu tenir lieu de station pour observer
une halte, et de là voir se perdre dans leur conflit
et leur collision, sphères, désirs infigurés,
peut-être même voir résorbées les épactes liées
à des lunes révolues ou restées au diapason
d'un soleil encore sourd des fractures du néant
et consubstantiel au vertige du langage.

At times it happens that this scattered space,
all intermittent in its aquatic shimmering,
seems out of reach. You imagine
that it might have served as a
stopping point, and from there to see spheres,
unfigured desires lose themselves in their conflict and collision,
perhaps even see the resorption of leap days linked
to moons gone by or still in tune
with a sun still deaf from the fractures of nothingness
and consubstantial with the vertigo of language.

Peut-être aussi que ce versant iodé du réel
par intermèdes en extension participe-t-il
de quelque remembrance, du jeu perpétuel
entre franges d'écume et effets isolés de lueurs,
sinon d'une fin du monde tellement ralentie
si chargée d'émotions natales que, parvenu
au large de sa propre chronique, on y est
ramené à tous les commencements on a
une ombre propagée en périmètre paradoxal
et comme incrustée dans l'élément des récifs.

It's also possible that this iodized slope of the real
resembles through expanding interludes
some remembrance, the perpetual game
between fringes of foam and isolated gleaming effects,
if not an end of the world so slowed down
so charged with birth emotions that, having arrived
at the open sea of its own chronicle, you are brought
back there to all beginnings your shadow
cast as a paradoxical perimeter
as if embedded in the substance of the reefs.

La séparation s'est produite quand la lumière
astreinte à la moitié du ciel avait fait du site
une instance déchue, lui avait substitué
un lieu d'exil, un rivage où le promeneur
en une sortie hors du moi avait reconnu
répercuté dans l'écho perdu d'une lointaine
lamentation, l'appel de son nom.
                                    Il s'abstint
d'y répondre. Mais il s'était souvent surpris à songer
à une rive mitoyenne où il aurait bien pu avoir
demeure existence visage et pierre tombale.

The separation occurred when the light
constrained to half the sky made the site
into a waning instance, had substituted for it
a place of exile, a coastline where the wayfarer
in a departure from the ego had recognized
reverberating in the lost echo of a far-off
lamentation, the calling of his name.
                          He abstained
from responding. But he often caught himself dreaming
of an adjoining shore where he may well have had
home existence face and tombstone.

La lumière par son ambivalence semblait être
réplique amplifiée d'une autre lumière
intérieurement éprouvée comme vicissitude d'ombre.
On avait cru l'océan échu à un immense au-delà
sur le point de reprendre comme à l'origine
ce nom crépusculaire qui a toujours été sien
et en passe avec cette dénomination perdue
de retrouver la faculté de faire revenir vers nous
rêveries dispersées pensées errantes
à tout moment sous forme de destin.

The light through its ambivalence seemed
another light's amplified reply
experienced inwardly as shadowy vicissitude.
We'd believed the ocean fallen to an immense beyond
about to take up again as at the beginning
this crepuscular name that had always been its own
and on the point with this lost denomination
of regaining the ability to bring back to us
dispersed reveries errant thoughts
at every moment in the form of destiny.

C'est là qu'une entité tour à tour voilée et diaphane
et alors qu'elle esquissait des contours
d'une subtilité de tracé qui atteignait
à ciel ouvert, en espace autant qu'en sensation,
ses frontières mystiques a dit : – c'est moi et ce n'est pas moi.
Toute la nuit durant elle convia aux mots
de rupture d'effacement de nuée changeante
elle rappelait que la mer dans son flux et reflux
était abstraction alternée, analogie continuelle
avec l'image d'une femme absente.

That's where an entity by turns veiled and diaphanous
and while it sketched outlines
with such subtle tracing that reached
in the open sky, of space and of sensation,
its mystic boundaries said: – it is I and it is not I.
Throughout the night it called upon words
of rupture erasure cloudy change
it recalled that the sea in its ebb and flow
consisted of alternate abstractions, a continual analogy
with the image of an absent woman.

Aujourd'hui, de quelque côté qu'on vienne
l'endroit est comme dominé d'une étoile dansante.
Il expose aux écarts des conjonctions astrales
à des destinations éparses il renvoie sans cesse
au souvenir d'y avoir béni l'aube à son lever
dans l'idée qu'elle était la première à poindre
au cœur d'une strophe sauvage. Il se pose
environné de vestiges où le moi se pulvérise
repères que l'imagination grandit et poétise
dans mille choses auxquelles nous renonçons.

Today, from whatever side one approaches
the place seems dominated by a dancing star.
It exposes astral conjunctions to the stray paths
to scattered destinations it refers constantly
to the memory of having blessed the dawn at its arising
with the idea that it was the first to appear
at the heart of an untamed stanza. It alights
surrounded by vestiges where the ego is demolished
bearings that the imagination enlarges and poetizes
in a thousand things we renounce.

Tout ce qui entretenait ici une image
de parvis imprégné du prologue de la rosée,
avancé en apesanteur pour donner asile
à une présence qui s'incarne parfois
au bout de soi-même en lotus empourpré,
a été dispersé, s'est confondu à la trame océane ;
il n'en est resté qu'un legs de mots nourris
d'effets de temps dilaté de distance qui se nie,
qui n'en finissent pas de regarder en nous
de leur immuable et perpétuel maintenant.

Everything here that fostered an image
of a parvis impregnated with the prologue of the dew
advanced in weightlessness in order to shelter
a presence sometimes embodied
at its very limit in a crimson-tinged lotus,
was dispersed, merged with the ocean's weaving;
nothing remains but a legacy of words nourished
by the effects of time dilated by self-denying distance,
which do not stop seeing into us
from their immutable and perpetual now.

C'est là que se révèle dans toute son étendue
aux prises avec les ombres et comme soumise
à d'étranges et concordantes fatalités d'itinéraire,
la pleine démonstration des retours imaginés.
Elle s'assortit de confins pâles et bleus entremêlés,
d'un promontoire à peine réfracté où les jours
sont incernables, puis d'un autre terre-plein
dans le recul où apparaître et au bord duquel
mitoyen à d'autres présences muettes on sent
sa lente résorption dans une brise initiale.

There, the whole parade of imagined returns
is revealed to the fullest possible extent
grappling with shadows and as if subject
to the strange and concordant fatalities of itinerary.
It includes interwoven borders pale and blue
a barely refracted promontory where days
are undefinable, then another embankment
in the distance where appearing and on the edge of which
adjoining other mute presences one feels
one's slow resorption into an initial breeze.

De part et d'autre continue le pays qu'on habite,
ses plaines ses brousses épineuses de jujubiers ;
une constellation tardive ébauche à l'orée
du paysage l'intercession manquante ;
elle resterait périphérique et lacuneuse
n'était la quête de cette durée perdue
entrevue un jour au hasard des routes
et qui s'est magnifiée en acaciée géante
imperméable aux variations entre le jour et la nuit
l'été et l'hiver, et en tant que moment pur.

The country we inhabit extends in both directions,
its plains its bush thorny with jujube trees;
on the landscape's edge a belated constellation
sketches the missing intercession;
it would remain peripheral and lacunary
were the quest for this lost duration not
glimpsed one day by chance from the road
and which was magnified into a giant acacia
impervious to the variations between day and night
summer and winter, and as pure moment.

TVI

BELLADONE

Mon regard errant ne rencontrait
aux alentours que l'uniformité continue
de l'espace aride où je venais d'échouer.
Rien qui interrompe le renouvellement
perpétuel du ciel du sable recommencé
alterné çà et là d'émersions pierreuses.

Pourtant nombre de fois j'avais cru
voir se lever dans le jour tremblant
des ombres familières : une maison grise
derrière un dais d'arbres, un enclos
délimité de buissons épineux, un aloès
majestueux voisin d'un sanctuaire.

Il y eut des moments où se profilèrent
transposées sur des plaines maritimes
fantômes, des images de scènes fugaces
que j'avais entrevues ailleurs peuplées
d'échos, de sensations et j'oubliais les noms
les dates et tout me devenait étranger.

Tout est absence de repère, dit le vent
en dispersant vers les débris noircis
de monts écroulés, les songes les mots
qui leur ont donné naissance, le temps
dont ils furent investis jusqu'à les assortir
à la plénitude de lieux jamais visités.

BELLADONNA

All around my wandering gaze
encountered only the unbroken uniformity
of the arid space where I had just washed ashore.
Nothing interrupted the perpetual
renewal of sky of sand begun again
interspersed here and there with rocky emersions.

Many times however I believed
I saw familiar shadows arising in the
trembling light: a grey house
behind a canopy of trees, an enclosure
delimited by thorny bushes, a majestic
aloe near a sanctuary.

These were moments in which images
of fleeting scenes I had glimpsed elsewhere
loomed, transposed onto ghostly
coastal plains, peopled with echoes,
with sensations, and I forgot names
dates and everything became unfamiliar to me.

Everything is the absence of reference, said
the wind dispersing toward the blackened debris
of crumbled mountains the dreams the words
that gave birth to them, the time with which
they were invested to the point of coinciding
with the fullness of places never visited.

Me voyant fixer un point écarté du sol
où perçait entre les aspérités rocheuses
une herbacée touffue à feuilles verdâtres,
à floraison rougeaude et aux pyxides
éparpillées tout autour, le nomade m'a dit :
– C'est elle c'est la jusquiame du désert.

Elle triomphe des lassitudes elle donne
au vécu sa durée en même temps qu'il est
désamorcé évacué aboli ; elle promet avec
les alizés une brise démêlant les bleuets,
mais on se hâte d'en éloigner son ombre
de peur qu'un enchantement n'y influe.

J'étais cet homme dont l'ombre exposée
insoucieuse de pareils aléas se confondait
à l'oxydation de la mousse sur la pierre ;
une autre présence ailleurs à travers le vent
au fil des mythes intercesseurs répliquait :
– Ne va pas plus loin c'est la fleur du voyage.

Seeing my focus rise from the ground
where an herbaceous tuft of greenish leaves
with ruddy flowers and pixies
scattered all around pierced the rocky
harshness, the nomad said to me:
"That's it, the henbane of the desert."

It conquers wearinesses it gives
experience its duration as it's
rundown drained abolished; the trade winds it promises
will blow enough to untangle blueberries,
but we hasten to push her shadow away
for fear that a spell may be at work.

I was the man whose exposed shadow,
heedless of such hazards, was mistaken
for the oxidation of moss on rocks;
through the wind, another presence elsewhere
in the flow of mythic intercessors replied:
"Go no further; this is the flower of your journey."

TVI

ÉTOILE DISTANTE

I

Elle est le diamant trouble de minuit
dans lequel l'esprit reconnaît
fondu à la plénitude du vertige
l'éclat tourmenté des veilles.

Elle est sans cesse démentie
toute en dislocation à l'aurore
lorsque tes enchantements s'évanouissent
et que tu empruntes une image
d'éternité à ce rocher muet là-bas
comme s'il était latitude de l'inespéré
à fleur des songeries.

Une autre image est cependant là
partout présente, en cumul narratif,
d'absolu murmuré de grande beauté et de perte
et qui ne veut rien promettre de ses voyages.

Elle est l'abreuvoir nuptial pour ton âme inapaisée
oasis hypnagogique et présence incidente
dans la bifurcation donnant par inadvertance
sur quelque emplacement déserté.

REMOTE STAR

I

It is midnight's imprecise diamond
in which the mind recognizes
dissolved in the fullness of vertigo
the anguished radiance of waking.

It is continually deceived
completely dispersed at dawn
when your spells fade
and you borrow an image
of eternity from that mute rock over there
as if it were the latitude of the unhoped for
on the surface of daydreams.

Another image is yet there
present everywhere, as narrative accumulation,
of murmured absolute of great beauty and of loss
and which would rather promise nothing of its travels.

It is the nuptial trough for your unquenched soul
hypnagogic oasis and incidental presence
in the bifurcation giving inadvertently
on some abandoned site.

Elle a des fibules aux énergies dormantes
des cordelières aux fils d'or ajustant ses étoffes
elle a des gommes qui parfument le thé des hôtes
et le pouvoir d'incrémenter
l'égrenage des merveilles
sur le ressort dérobé des chagrins.

Elle excipe d'un jardin
de pénombre comme d'un ravissement
pour répandre l'incarnat pathétique
de ses roses expirantes
sur la pureté de l'inspiration matinale.

It has fibulae with dormant energies
cords with golden threads altering its fabrics
it has gums that infuse its guests' tea
and the power to increment
the deseeding of wonders
on sorrows' concealed resilience.

It adduces a garden
of half-light as it would an abduction
to spill the poignant crimson
of its dying roses
over the purity of morning inspiration.

Et face au roulement des vagues
elle peut laisser effondré,
la grammaire en capitulation
et plus misérable qu'avant
comme au jour des lèvres nues
avec juste une touffe de fleurs
contiguë à son prénom,
puis renier toute étape océane
du suprême embrasement
au dernier lieu traversé.

Si c'est là le bout de soi-même
où donc a commencé l'exil
au fil des jours, et ce nulle part
récurrent de prétérit à aoriste
jusqu'aux sites pétrifiés du réel ?
Si une main fait encore signe
du plus loin des nues, des dômes,
de la distance bleue, de l'ocre
virginal des dunes – à l'éveil
où était le rivage annoncé ?

Et à tout moment encore
elle peut par durées interposées
d'un ciel ourlé de franges de feu,
de la béance du moi, en renouant

And facing the rumbling of the waves
it can leave one devastated,
grammar capitulating
and more wretched than before
as in daylight bare lips
tufted lightly with flowers
adjacent to one's name,
then renounce every oceanic phase
from the supreme brilliance
to the last traversed place.

If oneself ends there
then where did exile begin
as days passed, and this recurring
nowhere from preterite to aorist
as far as the petrified sites of the real?
If a hand yet waves
from the furthest clouds, domes,
from blue distance, from the virginal
ochre of the dunes – on waking
where was the foretold shore?

And yet at any time
it can through interposed durations
from a sky fringed with fire,
from the breach of the self, reviving

avec ses antiques attributs dédier
présent et passé à d'autres rives
au delà de la mer obscure
et laisser le matin aux prises
avec des transitions enchantées.

its ancient attributes dedicate
present and past to other shores
beyond the dark sea
and leave the morning grappling
with spellbound transitions.

C'est elle qui installe
l'exutoire narcissique
prélude à ce céleste entretien
dans toute sa coïncidence
avec une vision de l'au-delà
où l'on est étranger l'un à l'autre
et itération affligée de soi-même.

Elle s'occulte à la déclinaison
du verset de la limite
immobilisée en étoile distante
au-dessus d'un jujubier.

Elle a des mots sans fin
qui sont comme des bains
de mortifications
et qu'on a peine à retenir,
des mots aux consonnes oubliées
pour la dernière strophe
où vient s'enclore l'enthymème
reproduit au péril des carnets de route.

Et d'autres mots qui pourraient
continuer de flotter longuement
en diaphanéité sonore, tout près des tiens,
pour peu que ceux-ci s'animent
orphelins ou à demi sauvages
dans ta déréalité ininterrompue.

3

It is the one that installs
the narcissistic outlet
prelude to this celestial discussion
in all of its coincidence
with a vision of the beyond
where one is both a stranger to others
and afflicted iteration of oneself.

It is occulted at the declination
of the verse of the immobilized
limit as a remote star
above a jujube tree.

It possesses endless words
which are like baths
of mortifications
which we struggle to retain,
words with forgotten consonants
for the final stanza
where the enthymeme dawns
reproduced at great risk of logbooks.

And other words which could
yet float at length
in echoing diaphaneity, very near your own,
that they may come alive
orphans or half-wild
in your uninterrupted disreality.

4

Elle t'offre de ramener à la surface
par des effets de soleils noyés
et ainsi à une plus grande conformité
avec les lois physiques de la lumière
une à une les émotions préservées
de la terreur de l'indicible
du noyau âpre du langage
au comble de l'évasion rêvée.

Elle conserve comme gage d'ivresse
dans des coloquintes jaunes et noires
sous des latitudes improbables
la réciprocité d'une intimité à venir,
ton vécu diffracté en arc-en-ciel
sa rémanence en halo prismatique
avec la pesanteur du moi au repos
dans l'évagation de la psyché.

Un intermède aux confins du vertige
une heure incohérente et éphémère
aux abords d'un pays perdu avec
des cités dont on aperçoit à fleur d'eau
les toits en pente, l'ébauche des arcades,
coupoles en ogives et minarets triomphants
– tous ces monuments qui se hissaient
autrefois vers le ciel à présent engloutis.

4

It proposes to bring back to the surface
through effects of drowned suns
and thus into greater conformity
with the physical laws of light
one by one the emotions preserved
from the terror of the unspeakable
from the bitter pit of language
to the height of ideal escape.

It keeps as a token of intoxication
within black and white colocynths
in improbable regions
the reciprocity of a coming intimacy,
your experiences diffracted into a rainbow
their afterglow a prismatic halo
weighty with the self at rest
in psychic evagation.

An interlude on the borders of vertigo
an incoherent ephemeral hour
on the periphery of a lost country with
towns whose sloping roofs, arcade outlines,
ogive-shaped cupolas and triumphant minarets
we glimpse just above the water's surface
– all of these monuments that formerly
rose toward the now engulfed sky.

Elle associe au tumulte atlantique
l'idée d'un anéantissement suprême,
et le littoral à ce moment-là semble
comme suspendu entre les nuages
et elle évoque à partir de cette vision
en perspective désarticulée
tous ces ailleurs où nos âmes jadis
n'étaient qu'ombres vacillantes.

With the Atlantic tumult it combines
the idea of a supreme obliteration,
and at that moment the littoral seems
suspended among the clouds
and it evokes from this vision
in disarticulated perspective
these many elsewheres where once our souls
were but flickering shadows.

Elle a dit un soir prenant à témoin
l'ampleur du déficit stellaire révélée :
– Je suis ta femme à dominante d'encre
depuis ces époques reculées la même
qui revient en épouse voilée d'ombre
qui anticipe le désir de consolation
les déraisons les serments de substitution
au féminin éperdu et ressemblante.

Lointaine et cachée vers qui se tournent
comme au milieu des rues dépeuplées se tournent
vers une voix aux inflexions ondoyantes,
les souvenirs d'anciennes félicités,
un jour figurée en fuite de nuage
un autre incrustée dans la matière
frémissante encore des sensations
du dernier rêve en train de s'évanouir.

Tant de fois retrouvée ensuite perdue
quittée en se quittant soi-même
comme si subitement et en même temps
prenait fin la terre qu'on habite ;
la même sur le même rivage magnétique
au bord duquel en romance tempérée
confusément mêlée au bruit de la mer
toute chose près de nous venait mourir.

5

It said one evening taking the revealed
magnitude of the stellar deficit as a witness:
– I have been your wife of mostly ink
from those distant ages the very one
that returns a shadow-veiled spouse
that anticipates the wish for solace
the foolishness the vows of substitution
in the boundless lifelike feminine.

Far off and hidden toward which
memories of former bliss turn,
as in the middle of empty streets turn
toward a voice with rippling inflections,
one day depicted as moving clouds
another incrusted in matter
still quivering with the sensations
of the last dream as it fades.

Ofttimes recovered then lost
left on leaving oneself
as if suddenly and simultaneously
the earth we inhabit were to end;
the very one on the same magnetic shore
at whose edge like a tempered romance
vaguely mixed with the sound of the sea
each thing near us were coming to die.

Depuis que rien de ce qui fut ne se pose
comme étant réellement advenu la même
qui s'annonce en fiancée d'ubiquité
quand la ville retentit au réveil
de clameur endeuillée quand le ciel
est empourpré quand s'étalent
à la surface d'une élégie maritime
les grandes tristesses de la vie.

Ever since nothing that was alights
as having actually occurred the very one
heralded as ubiquity's betrothed
when the city on waking resounds
with mourning clamor when the sky
is tinged with crimson when
life's great sadnesses are spread
on the surface of a seaside elegy.

Il y a au cœur du monde
un chaos magistral une horreur
en passe d'étendre sa mainmise
sur nos existences confuses,
prête à ravager nos destinées
à l'image de ces abîmes flottants
forces démesurées et errantes
qui parcourent la matière cosmique
et dévorent la mémoire sidérale.

Nous cherchons la formule
qui l'accommode à notre désespoir,
nous arrivons par un subtil dosage
à travers une synthèse accélérée,
par une alchimie intrinsèque
bien comprise et bien méditée
et avec les mots qui nous restent,
à obtenir entre manifeste et obscur
des quintessences de remords
des syllogismes flamboyants
des redondances venues d'ailleurs.

Nous en tirons des fables médiatrices
où les préliminaires de l'Atlas
vers lesquels se lèvent nos yeux limpides
introduisent des parvis immatériels,
des terrasses de lumière qui invitent
par-delà l'étreinte de l'alphabet

6

There is at the heart of the world
a masterful chaos a horror
preparing to extend its grip
to our confused existences,
ready to lay waste our destinies
a reflection of those floating chasms
vast wandering forces
that cross the cosmic matter
and devour sidereal memory.

We seek the formula
that adapts it to our despair,
we manage by a subtle mixture
through accelerated synthesis,
by an intrinsic alchemy
well understood and well considered,
and with the words we have left,
to obtain between obvious and obscure
quintessences of remorse
flamboyant syllogisms
redundancies from elsewhere.

We draw mediatory fables from it
where the preliminaries of the Atlas
to which we lift our clear eyes
introduce material parvises
terraces of light which lead
beyond the grip of the alphabet

à venir consacrer aux absences
des préceptes d'orage et de résignation,
à nos rêves anéantis des idoles
dans du vieux grès rouge
tandis que les juges qui président
à cette cérémonie surnaturelle
ne reconnaissent aucune loi terrestre.

to come consecrate to absences
precepts of storm and resignation
to our crushed dreams of idols
in old red sandstone
while judges presiding
over this uncanny ceremony
recognize no earthly law.

7

Et ces tombes géantes du Draâ
que par d'étranges involutions
tu revoyais disposées le long
des effondrements tectoniques
des buttes aux flancs oxydés ;
que tu repérais sous une tutelle
de constellations grésillantes
au cours de tes traversées
saisi alors de strophes erratiques
de fulgurances et d'inaperçu.

Alignées dans l'espace lucide
elles portaient la silhouette
égarée de la lisière des rêves
à des confins de mélancolie,
dégageaient l'aire propice
à l'isolement des nuits lunaires
étendaient sur toute chose
un linceul de quiétude berceuse
procuraient le lieu qui dissipe
les craintes irraisonnées.

Mais pour l'âme suppliante
mais pour toi et pour l'ombre jetée
habile à rassasier de simulacres,
pour la promesse des chemins
pour la cohésion des fictions

7

And those giant tombs in the Draa
that by strange involutions
you saw again placed along
the tectonic collapsing
of knolls with oxidized slopes;
that you discovered under tutelage
of crackling constellations
during your crossings
gripped at the time by erratic stanzas
of blinding flashes and of the unnoticed.

Aligned in lucid space
they bore the stray
silhouette from the edge of dreams
to the borders of melancholy,
cleared the area favorable
to the isolation of lunar nights
stretched over each thing
the shroud of soothing quietude
provided the place that dispels
irrational fears.

But for the imploring soul
but for you and the shadow cast
skillful at satisfying with simulacra,
for the promise of roads
for the cohesion of fictions

jusqu'au pays où finit l'errance,
ces sépulcres à découvert
participaient-ils de l'immobile
d'une mise en relief de l'inouï
ou d'un surcroît de nulle part ?

as far as the country where wandering ends,
did these exposed burial places
participate in the immobile quality
of an accentuation of the incredible
or an excess of nowhere?

Le soleil couchant donnait au ciel
au-dessus des contreforts plissés
de l'Anti-Atlas et de sa cordillère
greffée aux préludes sahariens
une ultime carnation – celle
qui va passer de la teinte rose thé
à une rutilance de jets corallins
puis va déverser sur des plateaux
parsemés du vert pâle des éthels
la ténèbre des mers miocènes.

Il y a une troublante conjonction
entre cette pénombre enceinte
d'océans disparus, grosse de visions
d'orogenèse et la subite éclosion
d'un instant par où va s'engouffrer
jusqu'à soi le grondement des vagues ;
il y a du temps saisi à fleur de terre
en diaprures, et du temps régénéré
prêt à s'extravaser dans le vécu
depuis ravins et couloirs du vent.

Mais elle la coruscante, la culminante
la surplombante des glacis rocheux,
des yardangs et des oueds asséchés,
la constante dans l'axe du monde
solitaire dans son cycle imperturbé,

8

The setting sun was giving the sky
above the pleated buttresses
of the Anti-Atlas and its cordillera
transplanted onto its Saharan preludes
a last complexion – the one
which will go from a tea rose hue
to a rutilance of coralline bursts
then spill out on plateaus
sprinkled with the pale green of athels
the dark of miocene seas.

There is a troubling conjunction
between this half-light pregnant
with vanished oceans, big with visions
with orogenesis and the sudden opening
of an instant through which the waves'
rumbling will be engulfed as far as the self;
there is time grasped in mottlings
on the earth's surface and regenerated time
ready to pour out into experience
from ravines and corridors of the wind.

But the coruscant one, the culminating one
the one overhanging rocky glacis,
yardangs and dried up oueds,
the one unchanging in the axis of the world
alone in its undisrupted cycle,

sur un rivage ignoré des cardinaux
peut-elle être rendue aux apparences
ou sur un autre rivage du côté aveugle
de la langue être l'appelante auprès de qui
on se plaît à conférer avec l'absence.

on a coastline unknown to the cardinal points
can it be given back to appearances
or on another coastline on the blind side
of the language to be the appellant in whose presence
one loves to hold talks with absence.

9

Elle engageait à tout propos
une gravitation du sens autour
du sens en constant devenir ;
elle agissait ainsi auréolée
d'inaccessibles lieux de souvenance
chaque lieu toujours attenant
à un récit d'abandonnement
riverain d'une églogue surannée.

C'est le lieu auquel on a songé
comme à un domaine affranchi
du faisceau des méridiens
le lointain qu'on aurait voulu
rejoindre pour se l'être imaginé
au même emplacement qui fut le sien
et qui dut être alors si familier
au promeneur de naguère.

Elle disait c'est ici l'esplanade
où l'âme pourrait s'agenouiller,
où elle chercherait à atteindre
le pôle d'une cohésion étoilée,
où elle pourrait obtenir du corps
un appel de ravissement et faire
qu'il se sente dans ses fièvres
gratifié du bercement des flots ;

9

It would begin whenever possible
a gravitation of meaning around
meaning in continuous becoming;
it acted thus wreathed
in inaccessible places of recollection
each place always adjacent
to a narrative of abandonment
bordering an outmoded eclogue.

It's the place one has dreamed of
as of a domaine liberated
from meridian accumulation
the distance we would have liked
to reach so as to imagine it for ourselves
at one's very location
that must therefore be so familiar
to the walker of former times.

It would say this is the esplanade
where the soul could kneel,
where it would seek to attain
the pole of a starry cohesion,
where it could obtain of the body
an appeal for rapture and make
it feel in its fevers
gratified by the rocking of the waves;

et ainsi recevoir de l'océan
dans ses resurgissements nocturnes
vague après vague l'annonce induite
d'impérissables interrogations : de celles
qui sont riches en étourdissements
fécondes en durées séparées
voies de substitution à nos fuites
vierges des peines et des errances.

and thus to receive of the ocean
in its night-time reappearances
wave after wave the announcement induced
from enduring interrogations: from those
rich in dizziness
fertile in separate durations
substitute escape routes
unsullied by sorrows and wanderings.

Elle était venue en robe noire
puis d'emblée et même à son insu
s'est mise à saturer de chimères
l'hymne mettant à la bouche
en oraison jaillissante
tous les mots de vulnérabilité
tout ce qui restait continué
encore d'un chant d'innocence
préservé et en résonance
dans les sentiments irisés.

Elle avait repris d'anciens mots
chuchotés à l'aurore illuminante
comme au temps où le passage
d'une comète à l'endroit même
présidait à des mots analogues
envahis de l'esprit de la mer
égarés et à substance dispersée
tant ils se réduisaient navrés
dans l'obscurité de leur refuge
à un murmure exténué.

Elle est au large de l'à présent
dispensatrice de durée orpheline
sur toute l'étendue de son recul
prodigue en corrélations ambiguës
en connivences à demi étouffées

It had come in a black dress
then straightaway even unwittingly
began to saturate the hymn
with chimera bringing to the mouth
like gushing prayer
every word of vulnerability
all that yet remained underway
from a song of innocence
preserved and resonating
in iridescent feelings.

It had revived ancient words
whispered at illuminant daybreak
as in the past when a comet
passing over the very spot
watched over analogous words
invaded by the spirit of the sea
lost and of substance dispersed
so reduced were they distressed
in the darkness of their refuge
to an exhausted murmur.

It is offshore of the at present
dispenser of orphan duration
on the entire range of its backward movement
extravagant in ambiguous correlations
in half stifled complicities

la même aux parures de sequins
à la voix mélodieuse et dissolvante
la même chaque fois renaissante
dans la marge du ressouvenir
et regardant au-delà de la nuit.

the same with sequined finery
with the melodious dissolving voice
the same born each time again
in the margin of remembering
and gazing beyond night.

GB

LES SEPT VAGUES

La première à se mouvoir éveille au large de nous-mêmes
un tumulte de vague comparable
une sœur aînée en extravagance éruptive et intensité raisonnée.
La première pour être échue au souffle du vent en train de naître
la première parce que les anciens qui prophétisaient par l'eau
recueillaient des résidus à partir de son écume sèche
et pouvaient voir ensemble s'y réfléchir et s'évanouir les origines.
La première parce qu'elle respire comme respire en nous
la tutelle de ces mères souveraines
ordonnatrices de notre proximité effarée
comme respire l'allitération effusive et étranglée
tout comme sa syntaxe en diagonale de désarroi
et l'exercice de son atteinte fondue
à la trame nocturne de la chair ;
tour à tour éclatante purpurine somme des crépuscules
le matin comme gage d'une révélation muette
le soir pour une pleine mesure de questions bouleversantes.

SEVEN WAVES

The first to gain momentum awakens a comparable tumult
in the open sea of ourselves
an older sister in eruptive extravagance and meaningful intensity.
The first to come forward at the nascent whisper of wind
the first because the ancients who used water in their prophecies
collected residue from her dried foam
and all saw origins reflecting and dissipating there.
The first because she breathes as the teachings
of those sovereign mothers breathe in us
architects of our appalled proximity
as effusive and strangled alliteration breathes
just like their syntax diagonally in disarray
and the work toward their attainment dissolved
into the nocturnal web of flesh;
turn by turn brilliant purpurine summons dawns and dusks
mornings for the promise of a mute revelation
evenings for a full measure of earthshaking questions.

La suivante est sa jumelle tout aussi clairvoyante
reconnaissable à marée haute par son thème intercesseur.
Près des flots de la mer qu'on dit de ténèbres
pour son soleil déclinant aussitôt relayé par la lune qui se lève
qui s'étend jusqu'aux confins d'absence parvient
à une extrémité éparse de divagation dirigée
vers ce qui se perd et s'anéantit,
elle s'énonce telle une promesse de redonner
aux choses de la terre leur écho qui n'était plus.

Elle convoque les ombres qui se lèvent
dégage de la brume la présence
d'un étrange promeneur qui conserve
en émanation aurorale en manifestation
culminante de son être usurpé
à la main une rose blanche.
                            J'ai vu cet homme.
Il lui dédiait comme à tout l'océan
par l'entremise d'une imagination enfiévrée,
un cantique depuis le parapet où il mettait
sa suprême désaffection à l'égard du monde
sa totale répugnance pour le nombre de certitudes
alliées au dispositif de tant d'impostures,
toute la chronique motivée de la multitude de ses incompatibilités
autant de désaveux que d'exécrations en une démonstration
de peine d'effusions exaltées et de courroux.

The next is her equally clarivoyant twin
recognizable at high tide by her intercessional theme.
Near the sea waves called shadows
as quickly relayed by the setting sun as by the rising moon
whosoever strives for the extremes of absence arrives
at a stray extremity of drift directed
toward the lost and annihilated,
she enunciates as such a promise to return
to earthly things their former echo.

She convokes the rising shadows
from the fog extracts the presence
of a strange perambulator who preserves
in an auroral emanation in a culminating
demonstration his usurped being
with a white rose in hand.
                                        I've seen this man.
He dedicated to her as to the whole ocean
by the intercession of a feverish imagination
a hymn from the parapet where he placed
his supreme disaffection in regard to the world
his total repugnance for the number of certainties
allied to the array of so many deceptions,
the whole chronicle motivated by the multitude of his contradictions
as many disavowals as execrations in a demonstration
of a punishment of exalted effusions and wrath.

Pour lui comme pour nous
entre oubli et mémoire entre nulle part et vide de l'étendue
que reste-t-il des jours passés de leur complainte d'île déserte
ces jours imaginés et si proches qui n'ait été jusqu'au bout
intimité avec les mots d'une époque agonisante.

For him as for us
between forgetting and memory between nowhere and the vast
emptiness what remains of days gone by of their desert island
lament those days imagined and so close that were not quite
intimacy with the words of an dying era.

Vienne la troisième la bien-aimée distante
et qu'elle se retire peu après dans la cité qu'elle habite sous la
    mer.
Elle sait à quel moment il faut qu'elle donne
l'exil en partage avant de donner des rêves.
Elle sait l'heure exquise où les collines au couchant
portent la hampe des agaves vers une incubation d'étoiles.
Et cependant que son eau se sature d'éclat émeraude
que sa nappe entière se transfigure
et tandis que le voisinage est saisi dans la vision médiumnique
d'une Hespéride s'éloignant de ses jardins quittant toutes ses
    parures
pour se répandre face à la houle en longs monologues,
elle sait qu'elle expose ainsi l'âme craintive
aux images des grandes profondeurs,
qu'elle l'expose à travers un limon d'échinodermes
à la matière des sédiments où le corps a tout le loisir
d'aspirer à la nécessaire acquisition
de son élément incorruptible.
Elle sait qu'il y a aussi ce chemin en contrebas
tel un sentier d'attrition où la détresse à nos côtés
chuchotait longtemps au crépuscule.
C'est la sainte survolée d'une mouette rieuse,
à la brûlure des serments qui oppose tout un tribut d'errance
en rémission le point extrême de la méditation pétrifiante.

The third comes along the distant beloved
and retires shortly thereafter into the city where she lives under
the sea.
She knows when to grant
joint exile before granting dreams.
She knows the exquisite hour when the hills at sunset
carry the agave flagpole toward an incubation of stars.
And though her water swells with emerald radiance
though her whole surface is transfigured
and though the neighborhood is seized by a medium-like vision
of a Hesperid departing her gardens taking off all her
jewels
in order to spread herself out in long monologues before the surge,
she knows she thus exposes the fearful soul
to images of the great depths,
that she exposes it through a silt of echinoderms
to sedimentary matter through which the body may leisurely
aspire to the necessary acquisition
of its incorruptible element.
She also knows about that path below
a path of attrition where the distress that accompanied us
whispered a long moment at dusk.
She is the saint flown over by a laughing seagull,
at the burning of the sermons who opposes a whole tribute of
errancy the extreme point of petrifying meditation in remission.

La quatrième progresse en cohésion
avec une ultime apostrophe de siècle finissant.
Plus que toute autre fondue au récitatif
qui s'engage d'un vocable erratique
dispersé aux quatre points cardinaux de sa stupeur,
qui procède d'un abîme de souvenance
d'une fugue intempestive du moi
d'une phrase de déchirure dont l'ascendant obscurcit le ciel
à l'égal de cet arbre prodigue de tant de merveilles simulées
et dont l'ombrage fabuleux invite au songe
alors qu'il prédestine au néant.

Elle se renouvelle et se brise
écumante sur le récif s'enchaîne
au-delà de toute pensée cohérente ;
elle préserve ainsi contre l'absorption
intégrale et définitive la dévoration
corps et âme par cette mélodie suave
en continuelle protestation aimante
et qui retient si longtemps captif.

Elle est sous-jacente en échos sourds
dans la plaine nue dallée de pierre noire
un sol qui s'établit comme prélude
à la terre jamais atteinte
où pourront se consumer ce qui reste
de nom de filiation et de voies d'appartenance.

The fourth progresses cohesively
with a final apostrophe to the ending century.
Merged more than all others into the recitative
engages an erratic term
scattered to the four directions of her stupor,
proceeding from an abyss of remembering
an untimely flight of the ego
a rending phrase whose ascendancy obscures the sky
just like that prodigious tree of so many simulated marvels
whose fabulous shade invites one to dream
even though it predestines nothingness.

She begins again and breaks
foaming on the reef arrives over again
beyond all coherent thought;
and so she preserves body and soul
from integral and definitive absorption
by that gentle devouring melody
continually magnetically professed
that captivates for such a long time.

She is implicit in deaf echos
on the naked plain paved with black stones
an area intended as a prelude
to a land never to be attained
where what remains of lines of descendance
and paths to affiliation will burn themselves out.

Elle n'est pas prière égarée c'est-à-dire
imploration qui adapte à la crue des larmes
toute l'étendue des séparations.
Elle place en perspective de délivrance
d'un sentiment de mal d'être mugissant et si absolu
que s'il était mené à un seuil d'accomplissement,
s'il se formulait en termes d'itinéraire et de destination,
alors ni l'éclat du jour ni sa rémanence
en surface comme en profondeur
à l'heure éperdue du naufrage des tendresses,
ni tout ce qui saisit d'éblouissement dans l'ordre d'une fleur
ou exalte à ses préliminaires au milieu d'un champ inculte,
ne pourraient peut-être plus jamais se regarder en face.

She's not a prayer gone astray, that is,
not a supplication that adapts the full extent of separations
to a flood of tears.
She creates anticipation
for a lowing uneasiness so absolute
that if were brought to a threshold of accomplishment,
if it thought of itself in terms of itinerary and destination,
then neither the day's radiance nor its persistence
on the surface as in the deep
at the violent hour of the shipwreck of affections,
nor all that which captivates with amazement in the discipline
       of a flower
or exalts in its beginnings in the middle of an uncultivated field,
none of these, perhaps, could face themselves ever again.

La cinquième circonscrit la désolation à la coquille lunaire
de son chiffre plus puissant que le destin.
À nouveau les dieux morts choisissent de s'incarner
dans des voix blessées sur la grève
dans des présages d'abandon de perte d'haleine d'élévation
de sublime défaillance au milieu de paysages défunts.
À nouveau il fait un temps d'exil il fait un temps de fable
il fait un temps à évacuer tous ses territoires de remembrance
dans un ressac qui confondrait l'eau à l'eau
la réalité à l'air la présence à la dialectique
de sa dissipation instantanée ; il fait un temps
à requérir de cette dépossession qu'elle induise
un autre temps en puissance dans une vague
unanime où rythme et ressort
peuvent enfin se redresser à travers une langue
qui s'apprend seulement dans la fréquentation du silence.
Une seule vague dite habituée de la nuit
et qui écoute quand on lui parle
qui fait du dedans et du dehors les pôles
d'une même abstraction alternée
autour du même chaos changeant,
qui subjugue de la perception contemplative
d'un nuage argenté comme un amas d'étoiles au berceau
sans qu'il soit possible sur le moment de dire si l'on en est

The fifth confines desolation within the lunar shell
of her numeral more powerful than destiny.
Once again the dead gods choose to appear
as wounded voices on the shore
as foretellings of abandon of loss of breath of elevation
of sublime failure in the midst of defunct landscapes.
Once again it's exile weather it's fable weather
it's weather for emptying all those territories of remembrance
into a backwash that confuses water with water
reality in the air presence at the dialectic
of its instantaneous dissipation; it's weather's for
compelling this dispossession to induce
another potential weather in a unanimous
wave where rhythm and resilience
may finally rise up in a language
learned only by spending time with silence.
A lone wave said to be a regular of the night
that listens when one speaks to her
that makes of inside and outside the poles
of the same alternate abstraction
surrounding the same changing chaos,
which subjects contemplative perception
to a silvered cloud as to a cluster of infant stars
though it's not possible in the moment to say where we stand on it

à quitter entre-temps l'ère du verseau ou du sagittaire,
si l'amour est sans espérance si c'est par elle
que chavire l'univers hors des limites de son mouvement,
ou si le cœur dans la poitrine près de se taire
est mis à l'épreuve d'une métaphore tremblante.

to leave in the meantime the era of Aquarius or that of Sagittarius,
whether love is hopeless whether it's through love
that the universe sways beyond its reach,
or whether the heart in the chest almost silencing itself
is being put to the test of a trembling metaphor.

La sixième porte son murmure jusque dans les rêves,
familière de ces antichambres dans l'émoi où s'opère
la fuite des intervalles où se prolongent
dans un compromis somnambulique
périphérie solaire en visions exacerbées
et sémantique voilée des parcours oubliés.

Ô la plus humide des filles de la mer
et qui infuses au contact de l'épiderme
tant de propriétés apaisantes sur les fièvres
initiée accomplie dans la connaissance de ces entraves
méthodiques face à la recrudescence des avanies,

puisses-tu aujourd'hui comme hier
faire contrevenir à ce silence qui se propage
à travers les mots qu'on nous refuse
et qui peuplent d'êtres absents
comme d'une négation perpétuelle de nous-mêmes
dans des béances vertigineuses d'écritures ;

puisses-tu aussitôt fermées portes et croisées
surnager en résonance au vestibule
d'où l'on a si souvent hésité à partir
certain de ne disposer toujours
que du même ticket de jadis
à destination de nulle part ;

The sixth murmurs all the way into dreams,
a confidante of those tumultuous antechambers where
fleeing intervals open up where
the solar periphery in intensified visions
and the veiled semantics of forgotten journeys
stretch out in somnambulic compromise.

O wettest of the sea maidens
who upon contact with the skin infuses
so many fever-appeasing properties
knowledgeable initiate familiar with these systematic
constraints facing resurgent affronts,

may you today as yesterday
contravene this silence propagating itself
through words that we are refused
that populate with absent beings
as with our own perpetual self-negation
in vertiginous scriptural lacunae;

may you as soon as doors and windows are closed
float harmoniously in the vestibule
from which we've so often hesitated to depart
certain only to be in possession
as in olden days
of the same ticket going nowhere;

puisses-tu préserver cette pénombre en nous
avec sa lune et ses étoiles tout en débordant
simultanément sur toute la terre ;

puisse ta senteur d'algue brune donner à la douleur
aiguë et furieuse sa force de désir
toujours inséparable de la voix humaine.

may you preserve in us this twilight
with its moon and stars all simultaneously
spilling over all the earth;

may your scent of brown algae give its force
of desire to the pointed and furious suffering
always inseparable from the human voice.

La septième est majeure de sa durée tant elle se marie
à la substance même qui a cristallisé l'océan primitif.
On dit qu'elle est dépositaire d'un patrimoine
de figures ludiques et fascinantes,
d'allégories insensées à l'origine de ces inflexions
de ravissement dans des paroles qui consument
et qui seraient autrement inexplicables dans une romance
en présence de la tourmente atlantique.

On dit qu'elle s'investit de la magie d'un pays
qu'on ne peut regarder sans s'empêcher de crier au prodige
et dont le peuple n'a que des songes
pour s'enquérir du caché ou se hasarder dans l'apparent.

On dit que 'Oqba toucha son eau du bas de sa tunique
et qu'à l'occasion sa foi s'étendit sur toute la mer
cependant qu'il y avançait à cheval en adressant
à l'azur de pieuses invocations ; que depuis lors
elle se fait miroir et inversion aérienne
et qu'alors les hommes que tourmente l'infini
qui cherchent à leurs incertitudes une voie
au diapason de nébuleuses à la dérive,
ont appris à transférer jusqu'à elle
de vague en vague le poids de leur solitude.

The seventh lasts the longest so much is she wed
to the very substance that precipitated the primitive ocean.
They say she is the caretaker of a patrimony
of ludic and fascinating figures,
of ridiculous allegories at the origin of those inflections
of rapture in consuming words
that would otherwise remain unexplained in a romance
in the presence of the Atlantic storm.

They say she has taken on the magic of a country
one may not gaze upon without stopping oneself from crying
out in wonder whose people have recourse only to their dreams
to inquire about what is hidden or to take risks in the clear.

They say Uqba touched her water with the hem of his tunic
and on that occasion his faith extended across the entire sea
whilst he advanced on horseback addressing
pious invocations to the azure; and ever afterward
she became a mirror and aerial inversion
and men tormented by infinity
who seek a way out of their uncertainties
toward the spectrum of drifting nebulae
have learned to transfer the weight of their solitude
from wave to wave all the way to her.

On dit qu'elle se fait réceptive
par une soudaine aberration de la lumière
à des présences intangibles,
qu'elle prodigue nombre de récits à venir
quantité de narrations posthumes
et qu'à l'heure des multiples effacements
avant qu'elle n'ait touché la grève,
il y a une voix qui parcourt le rivage
et qui dit : – Tout est ombre nuage désarroi
et il y a des pleureuses aux bras nus
qui dévalent les dunes comme pour officier
à la mémoire de quelque nageur mort
parvenu là il y a peu au terme du voyage.

On dit à son approche : – Fasse le ciel
que reste intacte notre joie céleste
si jamais la raison se trouble et se perd le chemin
quand arrive à passer cette femme au regard d'inhumaine.

On dit qu'elle pourrait tenir au creux de la main
ou se retirer pour répondre
à on ne sait quel appel derrière la ligne fixée au jusant
donnant à penser qu'y émergent des côtes lointaines.

On dit qu'elle donne asile aux pensées inquiètes
et que gouvernée par l'esprit elle fait don au rivage
de la relation infinie des nuits à jamais perdues
des lieux où on ne peut plus aller d'un seul lieu d'épiphanie
à la place de tous les lieux de la parole à reconquérir.

They say by a sudden aberration of light,
she makes herself receptive
to intangible presences
that she provides numerous stories to come
a quantity of posthumous narratives
and at the hour of her multiple erasures
before she has touched the shore
a voice travels over the coastline
and says: – All is shadow cloud disarray
and weeping women with naked arms
descend the dunes as to officiate
over the memory of some dead swimmer
recently arrived at the end of his journey.

They say at her approach: Make the sky
such that our celestial joy remains whole
if ever Reason were troubled and were to lose its way
when this woman of inhuman appearance comes to pass.

They say she can hold in the palm of her hand
or leave to answer
who knows what call beyond the fixed line at ebb tide
suggesting that faraway coasts emerge there.

They say she grants asylum to unquiet thoughts
and that governed by spirit she grants the coastline
of the infinite relation nights never to be forgotten
realms one can no longer reach from a sole instance of epiphany
in place of all the realms of the word to be reconquered.

TVI

INTERVIEW WITH MOSTAFA NISSABOURI

GUY BENNETT: *How did you come to writing? To poetry? What lead you to write in French?*

MOSTAFA NISSABOURI: I'll begin with the question of language.

But first a brief historical reminder about this sensitive (to say the least) question: in the wake of the Algeciras Conference and the colonial adventure in the Maghreb, Morocco was occupied in the name of "pacification" from 1907 on by French troops sent from Algeria. This was after French and Spanish battleships shelled the cities of Oujda and Casablanca under a pretext that had been blown all out of proportion (as in the 1830 "Fan Affair" in Algeria) in order to initiate colonial expansion into Africa, as programmed by the generals of the Third Republic under Fallières, Poincaré & co.

The Moroccan Sovereign at the time, having surrendered and surrotunded by 5,000 French troops, had to sign a treaty with the imperialist power, putting the country under French protectorate for 40 years beginning in 1912. The northern part of the country was left open to settlement by the other colonial power with a stake in the invasion, Spain, which had also had designs on the country from the final decades of the preceding century. This region would appear on maps as "Spanish Morocco." The city of Tangiers was decreed an international zone. For the 40 years of the protectorate, young Moroccans in the north of the country were educated in Spanish and, in the rest of the country, in schools modeled on those of the French Republic and, after 1947, in line with the programs of Jules Ferry. In these establishments Arabic was considered a foreign language. In Tangiers English predominated.

But unlike Algeria, despite the occupation and dispossession of vast stretches of its territory in the north, south and east, Morocco never lost its sovereignty. And under the protectorate, traditional schooling was able to continue in established institutions as it had in the past (at the University of al-Qarawiyyin in Fez and in madrasas, for example). In the spiritual capital, Fez, as in other urban agglomerations – in the countryside, too – Moroccan children, myself included, went first to traditional Koranic schools (today this would be referred to as "preschool"), before enrolling in a modern French school at the appropriate age. There, the only subjects taught in Arabic were those like morals, religion and its practice, and a smattering of Lebanese and Egyptian literature (2 hours per week in all). When I was of age my parents placed me in a Koranic school where I learned several sourates of the Koran by heart as well as to write in Arabic. They later chose to enroll me in a Jules Ferry-type school instead of putting me into a purely Arabic school within the "public school" system (there were perhaps only two in Casablanca, my birth city). Aside from these schools, there were many more private institutions that espoused a pedagogy opposed to the one introduced and implemented by France, favoring Arabic out of nationalist sentiment and the will to resist the foreign invader.

So up to the end of the protectorate in 1956, we would see an entire population educated in francophone institutions (there was even a school for notable children) burst into professional life having been prepared to serve as assistants to the French colonizer – who planned to remain in Morocco *ad vitam æternam* – in the country's administration. Everything was in French, from signs, bus routes, names of shops and their displays, those of streets and cities, medical prescriptions, information sheets for pharmaceutical products, administrative correspondance and documents... Job offers were all written in French, either by the person him or herself, or by public writers that could be seen lined up in specific spots on the sidewalks with their Remingtons. Not to mention the press (except the radio, in classical Arabic of course, with time slots for dialectical Arabic and Berber). The only Arabic press was in the north of the country, and that with the permission – under certain conditions, to be sure – of the Spanish who, unlike the French, didn't care two hoots about a "civilizing mission." In the rest of Morocco, the few Arabic titles that could circulate had to do so clandestinely, on penalty of the relegation of their owners.

Since then Morocco has opted for bilingualism (classical Arabic as its official language and French as its second language), except in the courts and related services where only Arabic is allowed.

So what about my use of French? Vicissitude of history? Fatality? Intentional choice? Re-appropriation of the language of the other, the better to live my own status as one who narrowly escaped oblivion? It's all of those things.

I am bilingual (I've translated numerous arabophone Moroccan poets into French and when I receive mail in Arabic, I reply in classical Arabic), but French is my language for work, reflection, communication, and literary expression.

I came to writing poetry in 1959, if memory serves, and my first published poems appeared between 1960 and 1962. At the time, my poetic attempts worked the entire field of French versification, with a clear preference for the Alexandrine and the sonnet (the best teacher) with respect to composition. That said, those poems that were published were highly interiorized short texts in free verse, and they occasionally appeared in publications that were completely inappropriate but, alas!, like the journals that featured them, they have been lost forever. That first form was completely deconstructed after 1964.

I only ever approach the question of language with caution and I even thought at a given point that I had gotten past it, in the wake of Al Hallaj who said: "Languages serve to articulate words, and of that they die." Words wither as soon as they are printed (Gide).

GB: *What was the situation of poetry in Morocco at the time and which poets were you reading?*

MN: Unlike the novel and the essay, poetry in French was not popular with our authors in the early '60s. I knew but one francophone poet, twenty years my senior, who lived in Rabat. I never met him, but I believe he held a high position in the machinery of the State. Though he was well established in the Royal Palace, he was not an official poet but rather a carefree cupbearer, a refined amateur of witticisms as well as an esthete. He must have published a few slim volumes, but I don't own a single one. He was also a painter.

That was in Rabat, the administrative capital.

In the economic and industrial capital, things were different. A group of us young people in Casablanca, including Mohamed Khaïr-Eddine (d. 1995), who would gather for readings and to exchange texts, were sometimes hosted by a local association that organized readings in a café in the historic center of the city, or in the backroom of a beautiful bookstore in the same area. Aside from Khaïr-Eddine, who would pursue a career in France after the creation of *Souffles*, all those of us who "teased the muse" as they say, turned away from literature to take up less adventurous occupations. On the other hand, poetry in classical Arabic (and I mean classical, for there is a very sophisticated poetry in dialectal Arabic with its own versification and prosody, and which is a centuries-old heritage unique to the Maghreb) was available soon after independence via collections that began to be printed as soon as the protectorate-era bans on Arabic were lifted. In our group of young people, there were one or two poets writing in Arabic who would read their poems in the original and in translation, since there were both Moroccans and French in attendance. There was also an anti-Franco Spanish poet who read his poems in his own language.

But Moroccan poetry in Arabic, deeply influenced by Egyptian and Lebanese literature, except for the eternal love theme and the laborious exercises to rival this or that celebrity from Cairo or Beyrouth, suffered from the great rift that divided the nationalist movement and from the crucial events that resulted from it. In the years that followed, the Ben Barka affair worsened the crisis to the point that any reader could see that this poetry essentially revolved around opposition to the country's political regime. Despite a Machiavellian censure, it was the partisan press that opened the pages of the "cultural supplements" that one or the other of them was always publishing to both emerging and established writers. Among the many poets writing in Arabic, as opposed to this "committed" literary production, one poet in particular distinguished himself: though he spoke French perfectly, he artfully composed laudatory poems in classical Arabic and addressed them to the Moroccan sovereign (for compensation) in the finest court poet tradition, reciting these skillfully written hymns on the radio on national holidays.

In this hybridized context, my readings ranged from the Romantic poets – Hugo in particular, Baudelaire and through him Poe, not to mention Nerval (and through him Gœthe and Heine) – the Parnassians, Lautréamont, and Stéphane Mallarmé, who has never left me since, his *Pages choisies* with Guy Delfel's annotations in the 1955 edition of Hachette's classiques illustrés

Vaubourdolle being a volume heavy with memories for me. Khaïr-Eddine and I would recite from memory entire passages from "L'Azur" and "L'Après-midi d'un faune," or most of the sonnets by the Symbolist master. Valéry came later. That was also the period when we would feverishly seek out ranges of writing that would evoke the poetic in all possible texts, even the most unlikely, and we would occasionally declaim the opening lines of Marx and Engels' manifesto as if it were the introduction of a poem by Lautréamont.

There were also the "Zutistes" and the poets of the Chat Noir. For the moderns there was Dada, Artaud, and the Surrealists, Pierre Reverdy, and Jules Supervielle that I discovered in the special issue the NRF devoted to him in October 1960 and that I still have in my library. Char, Michaux, Ponge, Jouve, Perse, and many others I encountered in old issues of *Fontaine*, the NRF and Cahiers du Sud, purchased from itinerant secondhand booksellers. (There was an entire confraternity of them, including a set of twins that were impossible to tell apart.)

There was a secondhand bookseller in my family, and he would purchase entire libraries from those French preparing to leave after independence and resell them in his little shop at the flea market in the old town or deliver them to your home on his motor scooter. His address was popular with all the intellectuals in the Kingdom, as well as with an entire clientele keen to get their hands on a rare volume. He had a warehouse in one corner of the Casablanca medina, a real gold mine, where I would go and choose my books. Through him, from 1959 on, I was able to enrich my readings by other poets and writers from around the world (in beautiful French translations), whose works he would sell me for a reasonable price, given my status as a poor teenager; these included the German Romantics, Shakespeare translated by François-Victor Hugo, Dante, Coleridge, Leopardi, Rilke in Maurice Betz' translation... As for

American writers, in the early '60s I discovered the poets of the Beat Generation in an issue of *Temps Modernes*.

GB: *What did poetry represent for you at the time?*

MN: Excessive digression kills poetry. Suffice it to say that poetry was (and still is) for me a path to knowledge, and first of all self-knowledge; thus a path to salvation. For me poetry is also the place where it is acceptable to blend all fields of knowledge and whatever poetic qualities they may possess, which puts me in the company of César Pavese, who wanted the poet to also be the most cultivated man of his time.

GB: *Tell us about the creation of* Souffles *and* Intégral *both of which you co-founded. What role did poetry play in those two journals? Did editorial work influence your conception or practice of poetry?*

MN: Before the advent of *Souffles*, Khaïr-Eddine and I were very active on the cultural scene in Casablanca, particularly in poetry. We had known each other a long time, and throughout the entire period we saw one another our common preoccupation was essentially writing: we exchanged critiques of our texts, shared our respective discoveries. We were twenty years old. In our enthusiasm, we published a manifesto in 1964 entitled *Poésie toute*, a kind of literary oddity that was to become the first impulse of an intellectual movement that would prove to be irresistible. The title suggests there was an actual literary program, like those that came to light after May 1968 in France. It was more an act of presence, a still quivering, effusive speaking out in the midst of the uncertainties and questionings of the moment. Our generation belongs to a post-protectorate Morocco that wanted to access modernity and to be reborn in the world by the sheer power of the momentum that marked its struggle to end foreign domination, relying solely on the brazen manifestation of its eruptive self. We wanted to harness the budding music of our sensory universe to this energy that was submerging us with torrential inspirations.

It was the following year that I met Abdellatif Laâbi. This was through a French poet who was on a conference tour of Morocco and who was passing through Casablanca. One fine morning I found him waiting for me in front of my parents' house in the maze-like streets of the medina. He introduced himself to me (I knew the poet by name), and as I walked back to his hotel with him he said, "There's someone in Rabat that you would really like, and I'm going to put you both in contact." He did so rather quickly, and Laâbi came to see me in Casablanca.

When Laâbi and I got to know each other better, we discussed the possibility of a literary platform that would reflect our present day as faithfully as possible. We saw ourselves as belonging to a generation with other expectations, one that saw things differently than our elders did. We thought that the project, initiated by poets and granting a prominent place to artistic and literary creation, should also be based as much as possible on critical reflection. For us, the cultural players closest to this inaugural approach were painters, especially those who questioned the status quo and who wondered about the manifestation of an avant-garde in Morocco.

Laâbi was in contact with more than one painter in the capital, some of the most prestigious in fact, but after meeting one whose work stood out from that of the others we decided to launch the journal with the group of artist-teachers from the École des Beaux-Arts de Casablanca, the painter in question being one of them.

That was in 1966. The first issue of *Souffles* – designed in Casablanca and printed in Tangiers – dates from March of that year. It includes an introductory text, poems, and artwork on the cover and inner pages. The cover was not signed, the trend at the time being collaborative work. The designer laid out the name of the journal in such as way as to fit inside a basic, minimalist square, accompanied in its weightlessness by its lyrical twin in the form of a black sun. *Souffles* as handwritten in kufic script on the back cover appeared in the same pared-down style. For the contents, I provided contact with the poets, all from Casablanca, including Khaïr-Eddine who was about to move to France. Laâbi took on the role of editor, offering the use of his place in Rabat for its headquarters. He was the best suited among us for the job. In passing I will add that, as you can see by the format, *Souffles* is closer to a book than a magazine.

Strictly speaking, there was no organization or infrastructure typical of a classic journal. There never was, as far as I know: we weren't journalists or paid collaborators, and the question never came up.

At the very least, for the intractable dreamers that we were, all it took was an address, an authorization, and a typewriter to formalize on paper the – I would say impetuous – contents of a continuous inspiration, and of the imagination.

The state of mind that set in from the very start fully reflected this initial period of our respective literary adventures, an exalting one to be sure, and creative freedom was given full reign. You can well imagine that intellectual affinity was important, yet it was never to give way to the slightest form of complacency, an attitude that won over many a young author who published in the journal, which ran for several years.

The founding group was later joined by Tahar Ben Jelloun, Abdelaziz Mansouri, Abdelkébir Khatibi, and others... Throughout this entire time, *Souffles* was able to unite the voices of a group of young writers, intellectuals, and artists, and not only in Morocco. By opening up to other collaborators, it quickly became a hub of activity where the creative potential long waiting to bloom now did so brilliantly.

The country had been in turmoil for ages. Freedom, revolution, and progress were the watchwords that at times projected our youthful years toward a horizon of expectations, and at others restricted them to tenacious skepticism. Literature and politics merged to such a degree that the ideas we were drenched with constantly renewed the challenge to discover for ourselves the road that reconciles aesthetics and commitment. In such an environment, the duty of writing was to take charge of this equation, and in that, it took on an existential significance in our eyes.

Then what happened?

Souffles went through different stages, which were inevitably related to the maturing of personal experiences. The last known one resulted in the renunciation of the instinctive, disorganizing reaction the journal had claimed for itself during its euphoric (or heroic) phase. As was to be expected, this first phase could not last: since the publication was a visionary rather than an academic project, it seemed normal that even its hard core constituents would ultimately acknowledge that it had reached a dead end at some point and, in that case, that a critical reassessment of the undertaking was urgently needed. Having arrived at a juncture where certain crucial questions concerning current developments were beginning to be asked, the project had to find a solution by drawing on its own ressources or reappear in other forms, and so on. In that way our cultural project was revolutionary, exalting, always battling for the perpetual reconquest of its freedom.

The *Souffles* team began to drift apart in 1969. At that time Morocco was going through a dangerous moment in its modern history. Alas, it was to continue for several more years. For its part, *Souffles* adopted a more pronounced political stance as the serious events affecting the Kingdom unfolded. Less and less focused on cultural problems (it had published no poetry for a long while), it strove to give increased coverage to revolutionary issues in Africa, the Arab world, and Latin America, and to the cultural revolution in distant Maoist China. Beginning with a special issue on Palestine, the publication embraced new collaborators, and ideology – with schools of thought abandoned elsewhere (even by their promotors) and blithely picked up by us – gradually took precedence over its initial spirit of generous openness and discovery. The journal changed format and quality: from the transcendant, vertical form of its beginnings, it became rectangular and in the end prioritized Arabic. The initial project could have evolved in an interesting way, for example, by expanding publications with the press "Atlantes," which had brought out Ben Jelloun's first collection of poetry and Laâbi's first novel, in both cases with the collaboration of artist-friends of the authors.

Before the looming chaos, some of the leading figures from the journal's first phase – Mansouri, Ben Jelloun, and Mohamed Melehi, who were among the first to appear in its editorial committee alongside the founding group (which included myself) – decided, in 1971, to create the independent journal *Intégral* in order to carry on working without interruption, with Melehi, a painter, becoming its editor.

The right to an initiative being a right to a personality, I immediately joined the project.

As a reminder we shall note that the issue of culture in Morocco, in all of its aspects, was not and had never been monopolized in one way or another by the country's political regime – contrary to the other countries in the Maghreb and the Arab world, where the single party in power subjugated intellectuals and artists, essentially through authoritative rule, and controlled the means of expression. *Souffles* was created in this context, *Intégral* too, as independent journals, with all the inconveniences that such status implies and the vicissitudes which noncommercial publications of this type must inevitably go through.

Intégral would obviously devote more attention to poetry: the texts that would later be included in my *Mille et deuxième nuit* appeared there, as did Mansouri's major texts that I later collected and published in 2016 after the author's death. The journal likewise welcomed new writers from the Maghreb and the Arab world, as well as poets from France. Mansouri's beautiful French translations of the Syrian poet Adonis and many passages from the *Livre des Stations* by the great Iraqi mystic poet Neffari (d. 965) were also published there. *Intégral* folded in 1978 for lack of funds.

The fact that editorial work may have influenced my poetic practice at this time is not only obvious, I will say that it was even written in the stars: I was already prepared for it well before, as early as 1964, when I began deconstructing my first approach to writing. A concern stemming from an unflagging preoccupation with questioning (or from a critical vigilance), around and within the text, would remain a "constant" of my writing and my career. Others have been influenced by this approach – which may appear excessive, at times unbearable (is that not characteristic of the act of writing?) – yet also by the way my themes emerge individually as the text unfurls, and by the theoretically disconcerting form of my poems and the part played by the universe that they establish.

GB: *You have often collaborated with artists and even directed the École supérieure des Beaux-arts de Casablanca. Would you like to say a few words about these collaborations and speak a bit more broadly about your interest in the visual arts and their relationship to poetry?*

MN: As I said, artists were involved in the *Souffles* adventure from the very beginning. 1966, the year the journal was created, was also the year the Association of Moroccan Artists was dissolved, just two years after it was founded. The group of three Casablanca painters that joined *Souffles* had already been contesting the policy adopted by the Moroccan Fine Arts Services as well as that of other foreign cultural missions. Moreover, they had decided to stop exhibiting their work in these spaces, which they found compromising and contrary to their convictions. What's more, the École des Beaux-arts de Casablanca had gotten some attention, and quickly became known as an institution where the future of post-protectorate Moroccan fine arts was being developed. Under the direction of a young and enthusiastic pedagogical committee, the school began providing its students, who came from all regions of Morocco, with an artistic education that also explored the country's living (and particularly non-urban) artistic tradition, as one perspective of modernity in tune with the century and with the surrounding culture. From 1965, the École des Beaux-arts de Casablanca covered this seminal question in a special publication that ran until 1969, reporting on the research, inventories and analyses carried out by its teachers. The idea was to validate, within a cultural vision of modern Morocco, approaches and initiatives in diverse, unprecedented formulations that finally shattered the rigid ambiguities Orient/Occident, folk art/traditional art, naïve art/academic art – inhibitive if not problematic ideas that held the situation hostage to a purely artificial rhetoric.

A rhetoric popular at any rate with the then Minister of Information who was determined to oversee those programs more or less related to art, yet only to the extent that they focused on the promotion of local folklore and its corollary, increased tourism. This commitment, which responded to state choices with respect to economic strategy, was dominated by constant improvisation, and by the very nature of the activities undertaken, it fell within the previously reigning colonial vision. As a result, painting was lumped together with products that could stand alongside items from the souk and folk dancing troops without endangering their own specificity. So the cultural, aesthetic, conceptual, social, humanist and committed position of the Casablanca group could only have the enthusiastic support of the *Souffles* directors.

I'm neither an art historian nor a critic, but several artist friends have asked me to write texts presenting their work for catalogs, and I continue to do so, always striving to avoid the mannerisms and excess verbiage of those in the profession. On the other hand, I have collaborated with a few artists at the request of galleries that were selling their work, notably for an artists' book (*Étoile distante*), a portfolio (*Aube*, which happened to be the very first work in Morocco to combine poetry and painting), and an artistic accompaniment to *Approche du désertique* that was presented in different formats (publication, panel...). In addition, a fragment of the poem "Anticipation sur en exclusion" was calligraphed on animal hide, incorporating solar and lunar letters. I have also written two poems about two artists whose work had impressed me.

GB: *From the beginning, you have had a tendency to mix verse and prose, poetry and narrative, whether in individual texts (*Plus haute mémoire, Approche du désertique*) or across collections (*La mille et deuxième nuit, Divan de la mer obscure*). What is there in this writerly / textual hybridity attracts you?*

MN: A poem strikes me like lightning.

For me the poem never proceeds from an arbitrarily conceived theme chosen beforehand and predefined within a desire to write.

In both early and recent writings, I have already pushed the poem in the direction of what I call the "oceanic stanza," with extended breathing, and in which the lived, the dreamed, the thought and the unthought lead "eyelids closed to the edge of the absent question."

I proceed from an open, not enclosed thought.

The "dictations" increase as the text advances. In this I gain the freedom to integrate the prose poem, stanzas of a few lines, deep paragraphs, and on occasion narration (a tale, for example) in an attempt to better circumscribe this place of the word that seeks a spot on the edge of myself and even beyond. It is a single, shape-shifting text that functions in different registers, with its own music and in its own secret geography. Words are then forced into all sorts of unexpected cohabitations, into the most unlikely proximities, adulteries even (collision of eras and unheard of alterities...).

To be sure, what I wrote after *La mille et deuxième nuit* would inevitably be different – on every level – from that book. That said, the integration of prose passages into a verse poem is not my invention. Though there are passages in prose, they are not of the same prose as a news article, a philosophical essay, or a page of novelistic description depicting the setting where the Marquise has her five o'clock tea. The classic novel form has been totally transformed since the beginning of the last century, and what Proust, Dos Passos, Faulkner, Woolf or Joyce have done with it at times reaches high levels of poetry.

GB: *If your predilection for hybrid writing hasn't changed over the years, we do see a clear thematic and stylistic evolution in your work, from the socio-urban subject matter and occasionally coarse language of early texts to the more speculative themes and ornate style of your more recent works. Would you agree with this characterization? Would you like to say a few words about it?*

MN: Very briefly, as long as the aim is poetic, I make no more distinction between forms of writing than I do about the steps taken to get there. If I am more concerned with form than in the past, it is because the writing of the poem calls for one particular form and not another (rhythm, alliteration, assonance, more significant titles), though control of a poem is always only partial. In poetry, words are always stammering, ulcerated or half-wild, strangled words native to a consummate science of refusal: that of the exterior, distant approach that reassures us with its comfortable cycle of sophisms and overrated poetizations, that implies the interruption of any quest for meaning. Now, meaning for me must remain open. Thus my last work, which bears no resemblance to my prior writings, functions in new registers. The quest for meaning is not incompatible with the quest for novelty.

GB: *Are you currently writing? If so, could you say a few words about what you're working on? If not, how do you foresee your poetry in the future?*

MN: As I've just said, my poetic work in progress is not only going to be different from preceding works, it will be more fleshed out and divided into several parts (or partitions). I haven't yet completed it because it includes a project that I had abandoned four years ago and which I am still working on. The collection is *Divan de la mer obscure,* whose title alone could refer to Gœthe's *Divan oriental.* "Divan" is in fact used here in the etymological meaning of the term, which comes from the Arabic *diwan* and which means both "council room" and "poetry collection." "La mer obscure" is the name used in Antiquity for the Atlantic Ocean (*Mare Tenebrosum,* Sea of Obscurities). The unfinished text is titled "Station de la Dune blanche," the product of a chaotic journey made on the Atlantic side of the the Atlas Mountains and the Sahara.

Poetry will always be my preferred field of expression. But I am also working on putting together a collection of stories that appeared several years ago in journals. I have given it the provisional title *Miniatures pour la fin des temps*. I hope to find a publisher for it...when the time comes.

Los Angeles & Casablanca
Spring–Summer, 2017

GB

ABOUT THE AUTHOR

Born in Casablanca in 1943, Mostafa Nissabouri was one of the founders of the Moroccan journals *Souffles* (1966) and *Intégral* (1971). Former director of the l'École supérieur des Beaux-Arts in Casablanca, he has translated works of Moroccan poetry into French. His publications include *La mille et deuxième nuit,* a collection of poems previously published in journals and anthologies, and *Approche du désertique* précédé de *Aube.* He lives in Casablanca.

ABOUT THE TRANSLATORS

Guy Bennett is the author of several collections of poetry, various works of non-poetry, and numerous translations. His most recent publication is *Œuvres presque accomplies* (2018), co-translated with Frédéric Forte. His writing has been featured in magazines and anthologies, and presented in poetry and arts festivals internationally. Publisher of Mindmade Books (1997–2017) and editorial director of Otis Books, he lives in Los Angeles and teaches at Otis College of Art and Design.

Born in France and raised in Luxembourg, poet, editor, and translator Pierre Joris has lived throughout the United States, Europe, and North Africa. From 1992 to 2103, he taught at SUNY Albany. His many editorial projects include *Poems for the Millennium: The University of California Book of Modern and Postmodern Poetry* (coedited with Jerome Rothenberg), and *Poems for the Millennium, Volume Four: The University of California Book of North African Literature* (coedited with Habib Tengour). Joris and Rothenberg also coedited *pppppp: Selected Writings of Kurt Schwitters* (2004), winner of the PEN Center USA West Literary Award for Translation. Joris has translated numerous authors into both English and French, including Habib Tengour, Abdelwahab Meddeb, and has published numerous translations of the work of Paul Celan. Joris is the author of numerous collections of poetry and two volumes of esssays, his most recent publications being *Barzakh: Poems 2000–2012* (Black Widow Press, 2014) and *An American Suite* (2016). Joris lives in Brooklyn with his wife, the performance artist Nicole Peyrafitte.

Addie Leak is a freelance translator and editor currently living in Amman, Jordan. She holds an MFA in literary translation from the University of Iowa and has published translations from French, Spanish, and Arabic in various literary journals, as well as *Souffles-Anfas: A Critical Anthology from the Moroccan Journal of Culture and Politics,* edited by Olivia Harrison and Teresa Villa-Ignacio, and *Lanterns of Hope: A Poetry Project for Iraqi Youth,* a 2016 poetry anthology resulting from the project she coordinated for the University of Iowa's International Writing Program in partnership with the U.S. Embassy in Baghdad.

Teresa Villa-Ignacio is a critic and scholar who explores contemporary poetic interventions in ethical philosophy, postcolonial liberation movements, discourses of globalization, and social justice activism. She is the co-editor of *Souffles-Anfas: A Critical Anthology from the Moroccan Journal of Culture and Politics* (Stanford University Press, 2016) and has contributed translations of texts by Moroccan artists to *Modern Art in the Arab World: Primary Documents* (New York: MOMA, 2018). Her current book project examines the centrality of ethics in relations of translation and collaboration among France- and U.S.-based contemporary poets. She is Assistant Professor of French and Francophone Studies at Stonehill College.

ACKNOWLEDGMENTS

Thank you to Alain Gorius of Al Manar for graciously granting permission to reprint the text and translation of *Approche du désertique* in this volume.

Acknowedgment is also made to the editors and publishers of the following journals and anthologies in which some of these translations have appeared, whether in entirety or in excerpts and at times in slightly different versions: *Drunken Boat, Exchanges: Journal of Literary Translation, New Poetry in Translation, Poems for the Millenium: The University of California Book of North African Literature, Trepan.*

I would personally like to thank Pierre Joris, Addie Leak, and Teresa Villa-Ignacio for their translations and patience, Heather John Fogarty for her persistence and good work.

— G B

Selected Other Titles from Otis Books

All of our titles are available from Small Press Distribution.
Order them at www.spdbooks.org.